contents

welcome to leeds

Our local soap may seem overly concerned with sheep dip and sibling rivalry, but Leeds is fast becoming the north's most fashionable city. And like Emmerdale's viewing figures, it just keeps on growing, stomping all over the south's ridiculous drinks prices and treacherous transport systems.

It's no mean feat keeping pace with Leeds' ever-expanding social waistline, but thanks to this brand new itchy guide we'll help you find your boogying arse from your drinking elbow.

So what's to stop you from simply re-using last year's well-thumbed tome? Well, things are changing faster than the contestants on Countdown. From brand new bars to tasty new restaurants, last year saw a staggering influx of new venues to the city.

Restaurant-wise, Bibi's moved and reincarnated itself as an elegant Art Deco affair that'll take you back to the 20s, but without the troublesome prohibition – while Casa Mia made the move to the city, saving its loyal followers a £10 taxi fare to Chapel Allerton. The financial district welcomed new kid Tin Tin, expertly dishing out Cantonese classics to the be-suited brethren, and Bar Roc became high class eatery Anthony's.

Drinks-wise, the city continues to amply provide as if every night was Gazza's stag do. Norman underwent a suitably fabulous refurb, while student fave The Fav was adopted by the HiFi team. With a fresh paint job, DJ sets, live music events, and comedy, we can safely say there'll be a dip in the grades of this year's graduates. Newcomers include swanky spot Baby Cream, the Liverpool bar success that's popped down the M62 to Yorkshire.

Fancy footwork spread all over town, with Halo and the Quilted Llama's £5million church conversion opening up next to the university. Federation and Mission continued to offer cutting-edge clubbing, while the HiFi took over the Think Tank, promising to keep the alternative flag flying high.

In sporting circles, the Super Whites showed they weren't too big to go down after all, whilst Mr Alan 'Leeds 'til I die' Smith left for Old Trafford. But like a game of two halves, Leeds had the last laugh when the Rhinos became Super League champions by beating Bradford at, where better, Old Trafford.

There you have it, another action-packed year of swanky flat complexes, bright young designers, and underground jam nights. So, grab this guide, get stuck in and shake off those whippet gags once and for all...

two hours & two days

2 Hours in Leeds

Unless you want to spend 120 minutes in the railway station, you'd better stop wandering aimlessly and follow our five-point plan. 1) See the city – walk through Briggate to the Headrow, admiring the architecture, stopping off at 2) Harvey Nics to make like a local celebrity. 3) Nod appreciatively at the sculpture in the Henry Moore Institute, then 4) fawn over some fashionable designs at the Corn Exchange. Finally make your way back via Call Lane, stopping off at 5) Arts, for an emotional farewell drink.

2 Days in Leeds

Stay – Lay down in luxury at townhouse hotel Quebecs (from £80 per night), or for Art Deco design, the Radisson SAS is suitably stylish.

Shop – Hand over that credit card as if it belonged to someone else. Vivienne Westwood has eclectic fashions from the first lady of punk, while Space NK has top-line toiletries for your pretty little face. Visit Victoria and County Arcades for tasteful boutiques and antique jewellery.

Activities – The West Yorkshire Playhouse is the jewel in Leeds' cultural crown – big names of stage and screen regularly tread its boards. If theatre's not your thang, rock out to some local talent at any of the city's live music venues – Leeds University and The Cockpit and good for bigger bands, while Joseph's Well showcases the scene's new sounds.

Eat – The Michelin-starred Pool Court at 42 offers the finest a la carte cuisine, and its neighbour The Call Grills has a winning way with steaks, fish and poultry. For a lobster platter try Livebait, and for a Japanese banquet, Shogun Teppanyaki is dinner and entertainment in one.

Drink – Mook's cocktail list should keep you busy for the rest of the week – try their chocolate mook shake or fruity dib dab cocktails. New bar Baby Cream comes straight from the team behind Liverpool's superclub, and the Radisson's hotel bar is a stylish alternative if you want to talk not shout.

Club – Leeds' clubbing scene has never been hotter. Rehab and Mission offer decadent dancing well into the early hours, while the legendary HiFi Club serves up smooth soul to a hip and funky crowd.

2 Days On The Cheap

Stay – Despite having its own airport, brewery, and football team, Leeds has yet to gain a youth hostel. Still, Cardigan Road has a host of B&B's for the budget traveller. Try the Hotel Budapest or Butlers Hotel (both are around £45 per night, including brekkie).

Shop – Ignore those designer labels winking at you from window displays, and get rooting through those bargain bins. Headingley has an inordinate amount of charity shops, or head to Hyde Park for cheap and cheerful fashion from Sugar Shack.

Activities – For once the government's done something right and made sure most of the nation's museums are free. The Royal Armouries has four floors of deadly weapons, while the City Art Gallery and Henry Moore Institute have classic art and sculpture.

Eat – Get stuck into the lunchtime meal deals at The Box or Original Oak. For cheap dinners try Norman's £5 meal and drink deal (noodles, Mon-Fri), La Tasca (tapas), or Wokmania (Chinese and Indian buffet).

Drink – We personally like to advocate reposnsible drinking, but if you're planning to get as drunk as a shopping centre tramp, try Bourbon, Wetherspoons or any 'It's a Scream' pub for their super cheap drinks deals.

Club – Befriend a student (in itself, free), borrow their NUS card (again, free), then enjoy the disco sounds of university nights 'Fruity' and indie-fest 'Brighton Beach'. Alternatively, get to The Atrium before 11pm and get in for free, or drink as much cheap liquor as your stomach can handle and dance to the music in your own head.

www.itchycity.co.uk

days out in leeds

This Sporting Life

What: Dive into the city's sporting heritage.

When to go: The weekend's best for live sporting action.

Morning: If you're going to join Leeds' sporting fraternity, you'll need to buff up. Head over to Kirkstall's Virgin Active (£10 for a day pass). After the gym, pool, and sauna, re-hydrate with a refreshing glass of OJ in their on-site café.

Afternoon: You're a 10 minute walk from Headingley Stadium – home to the Yorkshire cricket team, and rugby teams the Rhinos, and the Tykes. If football's more your thing, Elland Road is still the home of local heroes Leeds United. After the match it's essential to deconstruct the game over a pint or two at the Headingley Taps.

Evening: The Otley Run pub crawl has the two main factors of team sports – it's competitive and involves excessive drinking. Start at Woodies in Far Headingley and see how far you can get without getting a red card. Alternatively, pull up a stool in the Sports Café for some hearty grub and TV sports from around the world.

Fashion Foot Forward

What: New York, Milan, London, and... Leeds. Get made over in the UK's latest fashion capital.

When to go: Mid-week for fewer crowds. Saturday afternoons are for masochists only.

Morning: Be inspired. Visit the Henry Moore Institute for ideas on structure and form, the Royal Armouries for antique battle dress, and Borders book shop for fashion mags from around the world.

Afternoon: Time to get shopping. For designer labels head to Harvey Nichols, and for vintage threads try The Final Curtain (secondhand Dior) or Blue Rinse (customised retro). The Corn Exchange houses the creations of local Leeds designers. Or you can D.I.Y with buttons, baubles, and thread from Samuel Taylor (10 Central Road, 0113 245 9737).

Evening: Suitably attired, debut your new collection at the stylish Call Lane bars. Newly refurbished Norman will complement your clean lines, while decadent Velvet is suitably glamorous. For fashion-conscious food, finish the evening at Harvey Nichols Fourth Floor Restaurant. Darling, it's so you.

restaurants

Hard Rock Café

The Cube, Albion Street (0113) 200 1310

This city centre rock shack serves up the same menu as Hard Rock Cafés around the globe – cheesy soft rock from a battery of TV screens and monster portions of Uncle Sam heartache. The service is ok (we like it when people are forced to be nice to us), and the food will satisfy even the most bottomless of appetites. If you're looking for a decent US diner that pumps out rhythms, has auto-graphed axes on the wall, and will help you eat your way to Meatloaf/Barry White/Har Mar Superstar proportions, there's simply no finer, or indeed, no other.

Mon-Fri 12pm-11pm,
Sat-Sun 11am-12am/1am
Jumbo combo £13.95, House wine £11.25

TGI Friday's

Wellington Street (0113) 242 8103
The waiters spin vodka bottles as they pre-pare your expensive cocktail and the rest of the staff sport Andy Pandy-esque outfits with oversized braces. And that, sadly, is

the best bit. The food's pretty average for the price, but everyone's there to stuff their faces with obscenely unhealthy fried things without anyone standing over them with a calculator and calorie counter. For some reason the majority of the customers seem to be celebrating a birthday. How many more they'll celebrate afterwards is open to debate.

Mon-Sat 12pm-11pm, Sun 12pm-10.30pm
Bacon cheeseburger £9.75,
House wine £9.75

Chinese

28 28 Chinese Buffet
Gower Street (0113) 242 6174

Nestling between the bus station and the market, 28 is easy to miss, but the people who go there know where they're going. Watch in amazement as they sprint in hungrily to gorge themselves on the all-you-can-eat menu, before wobbling back out like bouncy castles with God knows what swilling about inside them. Whatever it is they keep going back for more.

Tue-Sat 12pm-2am/5.30pm-10pm,
Sun 12pm-8pm
Buffet lunch £5.80, Evening £9.50,
All-day Sun £6.30

Maxi's
6 Bingley Street (0113) 244 0552

If there's one thing Raymond Wong knows about, it's choice. After a quick gawp at the intricate archway outside, and a quick paddle in the fountain, we counted close to 300 items on the menu at Maxis – 300! That's more dishes than there are seats... maybe – there were a lot of them as well. From the rich, saucy flavours of the Canton province to the hot and spicy tastes of the northern region, this is the ultimate crash course in Oriental cuisine. You could happily eat something different every day of the year should your bank balance allow it.

Mon-Sun 12pm-12am
Chicken with ginger and pineapple £7.90,
House wine £12.50

Maxi's Express
Balcony Level, The Light, The Headrow (0113) 245 7788

Skip past the tweenies comparing hair weaves outside the cinema and you'll suddenly hit this decorative slice of Chinese heaven in Leeds' newest shopping complex – The Light. Take your pick of the 300 seats and nestle yourself in between some luxurious fixtures and fittings for some eat-as-much-as-you-like buffet action. Those with bottomless stomachs can run the whole gamut, from soup and appetizers to main dishes, noodles and desserts, and all for £9.90 (£7.90 on a Sunday). Short-arses (well, ok, kids under 8) can chow down for just £5, so get your daughter to take off her high heels and lipstick.

Mon-Sun 12pm-10.30pm
Two main dishes from the food counter
plus rice/noodles £5.90, House wine £9.50

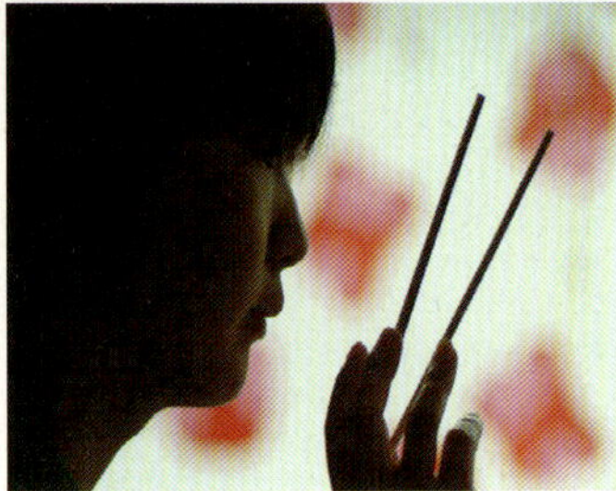

Tin Tin

**Minerva House, 29 East Parade
(0113) 245 1245**

The newest addition to the restaurant-rich Greek Street/Russell Street area off Park Row, bringing with it high quality Cantonese dishes and some bargainous set menus should payday be that chopstick length too far away. Dark wood furniture with a red and white colour scheme for the décor make it chic and modern, so you'd better hone your noodle winding skills so you don't soil yourself and the white tablecloths with spatters of sauce. The service is extra friendly if a little too efficient when it's quiet, but they serve great Chinese beer and wines, so we'll let them off. Up there with the best Oriental food in the city.

Mon-Sun 12pm-2.30pm/6pm-11.30pm
Malaysian king prawn special £10.80,
House wine £9.80

English

Anthony's

19 Boar Lane (0113) 245 5922

Yorkshire isn't renowned for its local cuisine, with the giant Yorkshire pudding being the most edgy thing on offer. So what the aver-age Asda shopper will make of Anthony's 'molecular gastronomy' is anyone's guess. Bringing science into the kitchen, head chef Anthony Flinn (the 'next big thing' in British cooking), mixes ingredients you wouldn't normally associate with each other. The result is a menu peppered with eclectic dishes like black sesame seed ice cream, roast duck with chocolate bonbons, and fennel tea consommé. We even saw the phrase "parmesan air" at one point. Needless to say, the Harvey Nics crowd has booked this place up well in advance so if you want to treat your taste buds you'll have to be patient. Oh, and save up – it's reassuringly, disgustingly expensive.

Tue-Sat 12pm-2.30pm, Tue-Thu 7pm-
9.30pm, Fri-Sat 7pm-10pm
Risotto of white onion and 'parmesan air'
£6.95, House wine £18

Browns

The Headrow (0113) 243 9353

Having never had a torrid affair with Charles Dance in 1940s Kenya, we sometimes like to totter off to Brown's palatial surround-ings for an afternoon of indulgent reclining amid the raffia chairs and potted palms. Appealing to ex-pats, the menu is typically British with European touches – with hearty dishes like fisherman's pie, steak frites, and sticky toffee pudding on offer. But despite

FIREFLY

21-22 PARK ROW   LEEDS   0113 243 1122

the elegant lighting and background piano tinkling there wasn't a whiff of decadence about the place, and we felt a little lost amid the 400-seat venue. Still, after our third sweet sherry we could have sworn we saw Charles Dance nibbling on our olives.

Mon-Sun 12pm-11pm
Steak, Guinness & mushroom pie £8.95,
House wine £10.75

Calls Grill

38 The Calls (0113) 245 3870

Forget all that blackcurrant reduction and fennel ice cream nonsense, Calls Grill serves up beautifully basic food that'll have your taste buds wondering why you ever ate anywhere else. Offering up prime cuts of meat, fish and poultry, their steaks are renowned for satisfying even the greediest of stomachs. Overlooking the river, it's the perfect

place for dinner a deux and the early evening offers mean you don't have to save up for weeks to enjoy the experience. The downstairs bar, Reclaim, will help you kick off the evening in style, and the whole affair is refreshingly free from all that pretentious Euro-nonsense. God bless Calls Grill and all who sail in her!

Mon-Sat 5.30pm-10.30pm
Sweet chilli and lemongrass chicken
skewer £11.95, House wine £10.95

Ferret Hall Bistro

**2 The Parade, North Lane, Headingley
(0113) 275 8613**

Proving that Headingley isn't just for student drinks deals and charidee shopping, this highly-rated bistro has been dishing out inventive cuisine for 14 years now. The menu reads like a Nigella cookbook, with unlikely pairings like pork and sweet marsala wine, red fish with pineapple, and chicken with lemon, orange and garlic filling its pages. And should your taste buds need any further stimulation, the homemade sweets include such delights as liquorice ice cream. A good range of veggie meals means even animal-lovers will leave happy.

Mon-Sun 6pm-10pm
Early doors menu: Sun-Mon 6pm-9.30pm,
Tue-Fri 6pm-7.30pm, Sat 6pm-7pm (3
courses £15.25)
Pan-fried rump steak with an aromatic
pink peppercorn and rosemary coat
£13.95, House wine £12.25

Firefly

21 Park Row (0113) 243 1122
Firefly's upstairs restaurant keeps the folk of the Financial District happy with a selction of a la carte classics and a less formal bar menu for grabbing a quick bite in between meetings. A sleek and chic interior makes for a swanky dining experience what ever you're eating, and they do a nice line in corporate and private entertainment functions should it be your turn to plan the office party. See Bars too.

A la carte: Mon-Sat 12pm-11pm,
Sun 12pm-10.30pm
Fixed price menu: 2 courses for £10, 3
courses for £12.95 (Mon-Thu 12pm-11pm,
Fri-Sat 12pm-7pm)
Brunch menu: Sun 12pm-6pm
Rump of lamb with aubergine and cour-
gette gratin, potato fondant and sauce
tapenade £13.95, House wine £12.50

Leodis

**Victoria Mills, Sovereign Street
(0113) 242 1010**
This swanky food hut on the banks of the River Aire boasts some strange things on its menu, but never having been to a rich person's house we just assumed it was normal. Visitors to this 180-seater brasserie can look forward to such treats as a 'deep-fried barrel of goat's cheese', which sounds like a struggle to munch through, but those who book for Valentine's Day are in for a real treat. For just £70 a couple, you can watch your meals literally shag each other on the plate, if the menu is anything to go by, with

delicacies like 'a twosome of sea fish inter-woven and snuggled together on a sheet of oyster scented fumet' and a 'romantic liaison of duck livers butter and garlic'. All very well, but ask yourself this: do you really need the 'lustful cream of carnal pleasures' squirted all over your steamy seafood? We think not (but we wouldn't mind a look at the squeezy bottle...)

Mon-Fri 12pm-2am, Mon-Sat 6pm-10pm
Fixed price menu: Mon-Fri lunch/dinner,
Sat till 7.15pm - 3 courses £16.95 (parties
up to 10 only)
Roast chump of lamb with chicken and
spinach mousse £14, House wine £13.95

The Old Police Station

106 Harrogate Road, Chapel Allerton (0113) 266 8999

Once the Chapeltown police station (and home to some seriously stubbly chins and tattoo collections), this bar/eatery could probably boast a pretty interesting visitors book if it actually had one. Former prison-ers can recreate that 'start of a long stretch' ambience by hiring the venue's authentic cell dining room for a small party of friends/ inmates. Food is more pot-roasted poussin than lumpy gruel, and being situated in the heart of the 'nouveau village' of Chapel Allerton makes this a refreshing diversion from the city centre.

Mon-Thu 12pm-11pm,
Fri-Sat 12pm-12am, Sun 12pm-10.30pm
Rib eye steak £12.50, House wine £12

The Reliance

76-78 North Street (0113) 295 6060

Owned by the same people that brought you North Bar, this nicely arranged collec-

tion of leather sofas is popular for Sunday lunch. Sadly, the clientele comprises of fash-ion spread wannabes commenting on how ironic everything is. The irony of this is, of course, that in a world where everything is so obviously ironic you can always rely on the bores of the Reliance to really piss you off by telling you so. How ironic is that?

Mon-Sat 12pm-11pm, Sun 12pm-10.30pm
Food: Mon-Sat 12pm-5pm/6pm-10.30pm,
Sun 12pm-4pm (brunch)/6pm-10pm
(dinner)
Goat's cheese and beetroot tartlet with
chestnut and thyme shortcrust and wild
leaf salad £4.75, House wine £11.50

Café Rouge

Waterloo House, Assembly Street (0113) 245 1551

Typical chain fare with a French flavour, so for steak and chips read 'steak frites', and ham and cheese read 'croque monsieur'. As a nationwide chain you've probably chomped on a baguette at one of Britain's many branches, and it's a reliable option if you can't be bothered searching for some-

where more individual. It's just off The Calls, so perfectly situated for the cosmopolitan set, but somehow it never quite manages to recreate that continental je ne sais quoi.
Mon-Sat 10am-11pm, Sun 10am-10pm
Fillet steak £7.85, House wine £10.65

No 3 York Place
3 York Place (0113) 245 9922

Housed in the business district, No 3 joins the bustling throng of contemporary eateries with a subtle French flavour, so why they haven't named it something poncy like 'legume' is something to debate over the impressive wine list. Food-wise, fish, game and poultry dominate the menu, and for those not comfortable with their table manners, there are secluded private booths as well as round open-plan tables. This makes good sense in the business district, because it appeals to those trying to clinch that deal in a big corporate slap-up session, and those trying to clinch their secretary in a big corporate slap-and-tickle session. Break into that expense account and think of an excuse later.
Mon-Fri 12pm-2.30pm/Mon-Sat 6.30pm-9.30pm
Terrine of rabbit with leeks and foie gras £9.95, Wine from £14.50

Sous Le Nez En Ville
Quebec Street (0113) 244 0108

How many happy hours have we spent whacking this place through www.freetranslation.com in a vain attempt at a witty gag? We'll tell you – many hours, many. If the absurdly convoluted French name isn't impressive enough for you, then consider that this place is actually inside Quebec House which in turn is built on Quebec Street – how more French can you get? Well, quite a lot actually because Quebec is in Canada. Anyway, just like No 3 York Place, the dining area here has many privacy-giving alcoves to those who wish it, e.g. married bosses and their voluptuous secretaries.
Mon-Fri 12pm-2.30pm/6pm-10pm,
Sat 12pm-2pm/6pm-11pm
Fillet steak with shallots, mushrooms and pepper sauce £18.50, House wine £11.95

The Olive Tree

**Oaklands, 55 Rodley Lane
(0113) 256 9283**

Believe it or not, your head won't explode if you venture out of the city centre, and if even if it did, you should head here anyway and forget about the consequences. A traditional Greek restaurant with an extensive, authentic menu, its setting in a stunning Victorian building complete with wooden floors, traditional décor and chandeliers make for an impressive dining experience. Owner George Psarias always ensures a friendly welcome, and if awards are your thing, he'll happily fill you in on their massive haul, including accolades from the Yorkshire Post, Egon Ronay guide, Relais Routiers and the Vegetarian Society. Live music will occasionally liven up your dolmades, but you really should be concentrating on the food – delicious.
Mon-Sun 12pm-2pm/6pm-10.30pm
Lamb kleftiko £11.95, House wine £12.95

Bibis Criterion

Criterion Place (0113) 243 0905
Bugsy Malone was an important cinema event for so many reasons. Children all over the land learnt the joys of splatter guns, flapper girls and the mafia, and personally we think the Godfather trilogy has a lot to thank Alan Parker for. And while your dreams of splatter gun ownership may never have come to fruition, the new Bibis is like walking onto a film set. Combining Art Deco elegance with big movie screen, this bustling dining experience is without a doubt our new favourite place. Unfortunately, our sentiments are shared by many, so despite its size it's always full, you can't book till 9.30pm, so before that it's first come first served, but with plentiful cocktails and a plush seating area, waiting around has never been so glamorous.
Mon-Sat 12pm-2pm/6pm-11pm,
Sun 12pm-3.30pm/5.30pm-10.30pm
Spaghetti with fresh baby clams £9,
House wine £14.75

Dino's

1 Bishopgate Street (0113) 234 4241
Dino's is usually busy – very busy – and it's quite large as well, and with the amount of mirrors that are banged on the wall you can easily get the impression that you're at the feeding of the five thousand. Thankfully, fishes and loaves aren't on the menu and there's certainly no bearded Big Issue-type bloke telling everybody how blessed the meek are. What you get instead is the usual sort of cheesy, tomatoey, pasta-type stuff served up by a legion of Romanesque blokes who look like they know the value of a good crucifixion. Hail Caesar!
Mon-Sat 12pm-2am/6pm-11pm,
Sun 5.30pm-10pm
Margarita pizza £6.50, House wine £11.95

Est Est Est

31-33 East Parade (0113) 246 0669

3E – as they don't call themselves – have somehow managed to convince a gullible public that they're classy, or sophisticated, or good for networking, or whatever they put on their promotional material to pack in the ABC1 punters. However, when you realise that these punters have been lured away from the likes of Pizza Express you'll understand just how classy and sophisticated they are. Est Est Est serves up a fairly short menu of dishes that don't taste much better, or appear more carefully prepared than their Morrison's ready-meal counterparts. And indeed, the punters in here tend to look like Morrison's staff who've won a GMTV competition for a makeover and meet and greet with their favourite soap star.
East Parade: Mon-Sun 12pm-10.30pm
Goat's cheese pizza with pine nuts and pesto £8.35, House wine £11.50

Pietro

70 Otley Road (0113) 274 4262
Far Headingley may not seem like a cultural hot spot, but whether it be Valentine's Day or a drizzly Tuesday in November, this local Italian is always rammed. They've instigated a few changes over the years – the rustic fishing nets have gone, it's now non-smoking, and they've hitched up the prices, but one taste of their giant calzone creations and you'll be a regular. We like the extra large wine glasses – if only because we could pour ourselves half a bottle of wine without looking like we've got a drinking problem.
Tue-Thu 6pm-10.30pm, Fri-Sat 6pm-11pm, Sun 6pm-10pm
Pietro pizza £7.50, House wine £10.50

Pizza Express

White Cloth Hall, Crown Street (0113) 246 520

Not content with infiltrating Dubai, New Delhi, and Kuwait, this 'posh' pizza and pasta chain has three bumper branches right here in Yorkshire. You know the score – tiny tasty pizzas and Coca-Cola in glass bottles.
Mon-Tue 11.30am-11pm,
Wed-Fri 11.30am-12am, Sat 12pm-12am,
Sun 12pm-11pm
D'Autunno salad £7.95,
House wine £13.95

Salvos

115 Otley Road, Headingley
(0113) 275 5017
Just four years after the Godfather burst onto cinema screens this popular Headingley eatery started re-educating the British public about Italian food. There isn't a bloody fruit salad, stolen cannoli, or horse head appetiser in sight, instead you'll find inventive Italian cuisine and classic favourites. The tables are still a little too close together – so try not to talk business over dinner – but with menu options like field roasted mushrooms, calves liver, and seafood stew, this culinary opportunity is an offer you can't refuse. Capiche?
Mon-Sun 12pm-2pm, Mon-Thu 6pm-10.45pm, Fri-Sat 5.30pm-11pm
Early bird (Mon-Fri till 7pm): 2 courses & coffee £10, 3 courses & coffee £12.95
Baked pasta with ham, meatballs, salami, and mozzarella £7.95, House wine £11.95

Indian

Akbars

Eastgate (0113) 245 6566
16 Greek Street (0113) 242 5426
Big-thinking Akbars began life in Bradford before introducing its 100-seater curry emporium on Eastgate. Now they've expanded to the old Bibi's site and have further plans to make it in Manchester. Egyptian décor and ornaments dominate, which gives the restaurant reviewer a pharaoh-ld opportunity of slipping in some dodgy puns. But we wouldn't do that. So let's just say that efficiency and value is the name of the game at Akbars where giant naans and good, cheap food leave you feeling mighty pogged without having to dip into your taxi money. There. We did it without any Egyptian puns at all because, after all, fez fair.
Mon-Thu 5pm-12am,
Fri-Sat 5pm-12.30am
Chicken dopiaza £6.95, House wine £9.95

Darbar

16/17 Kirkgate (0113) 246 0381

An opulent Aladdin's cave of traditional Indian food served up in a mural-strewn palace with ornate pillars and carved rosewood. At weekends they even have the Sultan of Bling – an impressively bearded gentlemen in turban and robes – who'll hold the downstairs door open for you, should you not have the strength yourself. You're advised to skip breakfast and lunch, as snacks are laid on pre and post meal. Tuck into a giant bowl of Bombay mix while you order, then finish off the evening with a personal bowl of exotic fruit. The only possible thing missing is a jewel-adorned elephant, but just think of the man with the shovel...
Mon-Sat 11.30am-2.30pm/6pm-12am
Tandoori king prawns £9.90,
House wine £12.95

original taste in an exotic setting at the oldest established Indian Restaurant in the Leeds City centre.

"the most authentic alacarte choice in town"

Complete your visit to Leeds by dining at the Shabab.

fully licensed and Air Conditioning

2 Eastgate, Leeds, LS2 7JL - 0113 246 8988

info@shababrestaurants.co.uk

Shabab

2 Eastgate (0113) 246 8988

Shabab may test the credit card more than many, but they do grind all their spice in-house and rely on only the freshest ingredients from local suppliers. Asian Choice Magazine obviously agree, and voted Shabab 'Best Value For Money' and they're likely to be the experts. The oldest curry house in Leeds and proud of it too, but a recent refurbishment has helped it keep pace with its imitators. The Shabab all-you-can-eat buffet is legendary but, before you ask, you can't bring your elephant, and don't try and stuff your leftovers down your trousers – those spices will stain. Child friendly and fully licensed, they make all of their dishes fresh on the day, making this handy city centre spot a sterling choice for the obligatory weekly curry trip.

Mon-Fri 11.30am-2.15pm, Sun-Thu 5pm-11.45pm, Fri-Sat 5pm-12.30am
Buffet: Mon-Fri 11.45am-2.15pm,
Mon-Sat 5.30pm-9pm
Chicken nehari £6.90, House wine £10.90

Spice 4U

8b-10b Market Street Arcade
(0113) 243 3737

Like a long-lost Prince track, the name and feel of this central curry stop are unashamedly 80s. Perched atop the piss-stained alleyway of Market Street Arcade, this jazzed-up diner is a modern alternative to its Raj-based competitors. Part of a Yorkshire mini-chain owned by the Miah family, it specialises in Indian and Bangladeshi food and is close enough to the HiFi club to exert a gravitational pull on its punters, who can't be wrong.

Sun-Thu 5pm-12am, Fri-Sat 5pm-1am
Chicken dopiaza £5.50, House wine £10.50

Tariq's

12-16 St Michael's Road, Headingley
(0113) 275 1881

This bright and friendly Headingley Indian recently lost its license – good for the already tipsy Headingley clientele (it's 30 seconds walk from both the Oak and the Skyrack), but not so good for the completely sober. You see, the orange walls and 100 watt lighting are so bright, anyone with half-decent vision will need to take the edge off. Still, the staff are friendly, the food fair and it's the only curry cottage in the area. Result.

Sun-Thu 5pm-1am, Fri-Sat 5pm-3am
Chicken tikka masala £5, Unlicensed

Seven Spices

203-205 Woodhouse Street
(0113) 243 5758

Refreshingly different from your average Leeds Indian because it's too far from a pub to attract late night drunks. OK, so it's only 100 yards from the Swan with Two Necks but another Indian has got between the two of them and as a result we're not recommending it to you. Big windows allow would-be punters to see the spanking new interior of this student friendly slop-shop, but the only reward for getting inside is a view of Hyde Park Liberal Club and a bus stop. While this seems slightly unfair, they make up for it with consistently tasty curries, massive naan breads, and lashings of friendly smiles.

Mon-Sun 5.30pm-1am
Chicken tikka masala £5.75,
House wine £8.90

56 Oriental Restaurant

56 Wellington Street (0113) 245 0380

Taking mimalist chic to a whole new level, this immaculate upstairs eatery is a potent reminder to anyone who can't keep their home clean. Just think, if the staff here can keep a bustling city centre restaurant this shiny and new, why oh why does your own kitchen look like a busload of kids with ADHD has ransacked it with machetes? Super clean décor aside, this is possibly the best Oriental restaurant in Leeds, with a menu stretching as far as Japan, Malaysia, Thailand, Korea, Vietnam, Mongolia, and China. The portions can be a bit on the small side, but dishes come garnished with fresh fruit and flowers, which made us feel all special. The bargainous set meals are popular but despite the quick, smiley service it can feel a little impersonal. That might just be an overthrow from our unhappy childhood though.

Mon-Sun 12pm-2.30pm, Mon-Fri 5pm-
11pm, Sat 6pm-11pm, Sun 6pm-10.30pm
Promotional menu: Mon-Fri lunch – 2
courses £5.95, Mon-Fri 5pm-7pm/Sat-Sun
lunch – 3 courses £7.55
Malaysian curry £7.95, House wine £9.95

Fuji Hiro

Merrion Centre, 45 Wade Lane
(0113) 243 9184

It doesn't take long to cook noodles and that's what makes this chow mein chomping house the Japanese equivalent of KFC. There are Formica tables and smiling faces everywhere as bowls and bowls of the bloody stuff gets thrown down necks of people who aren't too clever with the chopsticks with gay abandon. Cheap, cheerful, and chocker.

Sun-Thu 12pm-10pm, Fri-Sat 12pm-11pm
Yakisoba £5.95, House wine £8.50

Tampopo

15 South Parade (0113) 245 1816

Specialising in freshly cooked dishes from across East Asia, such is their commitment to getting the taste right, they order their veg all the way from Bangkok. A mixture of flavours from Thailand, Vietnam, Indonesia, Malaysia and Japan, there's plenty on the menu to suit whether it's a rice or noodle dish you fancy, and if you're feeling like munching on prawns in your slippers, they even do a takeaway service (but you'll have to get dressed to go and get it). The service is quick and friendly and the décor minimalist and clean, so why you'd want to wallow in your messy flat instead of pushing the boat out and heading out for dinner, we don't know.

Mon-Sat 12pm-11pm, Sun 12pm-10pm
Seafood yaki udon £8.95,
House wine £10.95

Shogun Teppan-yaki

Granary Wharf (0113) 245 1856

The Japanese art of table-top cooking reaches Yorkshire. Set in Granary Wharf, it's best for big groups so you can go for the banquet and have everything cooked at your table by some guy with a crazy flame-throwing grill. They tend to push this option, but those with small stomachs, or wallets, should know it's rather expensive and features enough food for breakfast, lunch and dinner. The chef'll invite you to join in (breaking eggs, not handling flames or anything) and before you know it you're in the middle of a bizarre 'reality dining' experience. Not quite as bad as the Japanese game show 'Endurance' but you can see where they get their ideas from...

Tue-Sat 11am-3pm, Mon-Sat 6pm-11pm
8-course special £26, House wine £11

Seafood

Livebait

**11-15 Wharf Street, The Calls
(0113) 244 4144**

Livebait is a posh seafood place near Calls Grill where you can, er...eat seafood. But that's not all, because there's also some special picnic bench-style seating outside where you can, er....eat more seafood. If this doesn't sound very exciting then think of the poor friendly guy who's been touring the working men's clubs and back street pubs of Leeds on a Friday night with a little tray of shellfish strapped to his chest for the last 30 years. Every week it's the same old story as boozy jibes such as: "Have you got any crabs on ya, cock?" and "Have you got any mussels – well why aren't you carrying too trays then?" fall on his weary ears. However, this is probably the way that seafood should be eaten, so head for the WMCs and give these cockles a swerve.

Mon-Thu 12pm-3pm, Mon-Thu 5.45pm-10.30pm, Fri-Sat 12pm-11pm
Bar: Mon-Sat 12pm-11pm
Set menu: 2 courses £12.95, 3 courses £16.50 (not avail. Fri-Sat after 7pm)
Seared sea bass fillet with ginger and chilli crab, baby spinach, noodles and hoisin sauce £15.25, House wine £11.50

Organic

The Mill Race

2 Commercial Road (0113) 275 7555
Organic is most definitely the buzzword here, but their quest to get the best ingredients from the best suppliers onto your plate in the best arrangement possible doesn't mean they skimp everywhere else. A small restaurant with a modern yet rustic feel to it, there's exposed stone and classic décor, and despite its out of town location, draws in plenty of punters who know what's good for 'em. A menu of modern British classics with European flourishes goes down a treat, as does the wine list, voted Britain's best by Les Routiers in 2004. An adjoining bar and smoking lounge upstairs mean you don't have to take the healthy living thing too far.

Mon-Sun 6pm-11pm (food 'til 9.30pm Mon-Sat, 8pm Sun)
Sea bass on fennel risotto with a balsamic reduction £14.25, House wine £12.95

Mexican

Cactus Lounge

**3 St Peter's Building, St Peter's Square
(0113) 243 6553**

Within spitting distance (but don't, it's rude) of the West Yorkshire Playhouse, the Leeds College of Music, and the new BBC building, this modernistic nacho shack is literally doused in talent. On any one night you could be sharing spices with anyone from Patrick Stewart to the next Jamie Cullum.

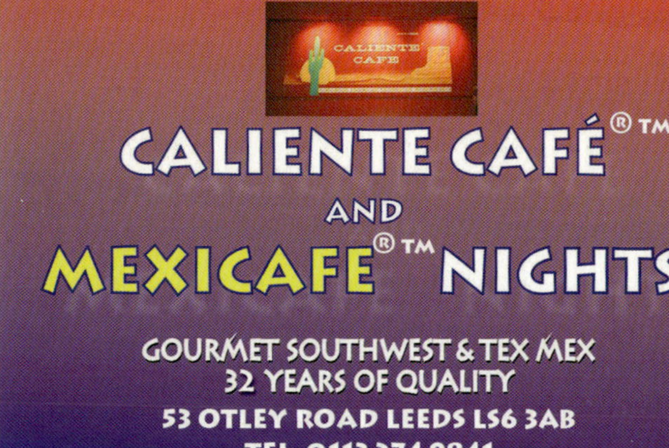

Arrive between 5pm and 7pm and enjoy a two course 'pre-theatre special' or become a frequent flyer with their discount Diners Club Card. Tie-ins with the nearby Wardrobe mean you can make a night of it by dancing away those Cactus Lounge calories with a bevy of bright young things.

Pre-theatre deal: Mon-Sat 5pm-7pm (last booking 6.45pm, tables may be required by 8.15pm) – 2 courses £9.95
Mon-Fri 12pm-2pm, Mon-Sat 5pm-10pm
Chicken hongos burrito £8.95,
House wine £9.95

Caliente Café

53 Otley Road (0113) 274 9841
With a restaurant like this in their midst, Headingley-ites just don't know they're born. Over 30 years in the business and a commitment to providing an authentic Mexican menu, they'll go as far as importing their chillies from Mexico and rice from Pakistan in search of the best flavours possible. Their Caliente weekend menu is filled with well-known Mexican dishes including enchiladas (the pollo mole isn't to be missed) and lesser known classics like queso fondido, with the diner-style Mexicafe®TM menu maintaining

the high quality during the week for £2-£3 a head less. An impressive wine list, selection of margaritas and scrumptiously sinful dessert menu will have you loosening the belt, and with an intimately buzzing atmosphere it's the perfect place for a lengthy meal with mates. Leeds dining doesn't get much better.

Mexicafe menu®TM: Sun/Tue-Thu 6.30pm-10pm, Caliente menu: Fri-Sat 6.30pm-10.30pm
Enchilda rojas £8.95, House wine £8.95

Gringos Salsa Mexicana

116 Harrogate Road, Chapel Allerton (0113) 268 1110

Donkeys, sombreros, bits of Beatles, spicy peanuts – even the walls are crumbling in authentic Mexican styleeee. You'll regret overdosing on the nuts when you're trying to wedge in your 15th build-yourself burrito. As well as incredibly generous portions they have a decent selection of imported Mexican beers (and on Thursday nights selected beers are a quid a bottle). The place is cosy (small) and atmospheric (dimly lit) and you can't book a table later than 8pm so get here early or late to guarantee a table.

The best restaurant in Chapel Allerton and possibly the best Mexican in Leeds.
Mon-Sat 6pm-11pm, Sun 6pm-10.30pm
Fajitas £9.95, House wine £10.90

La Tasca

Greek Street (0113) 244 2205

This popular Spanish chain link boasts pitchers of sangria and tapas as a speciality, but then again which Spanish restaurant doesn't? Claiming to be 'so authentic you won't find anything better in Spain', you'd be forgiven for wondering where, exactly, are the Ibizan all-night discos, lycra-clad slappers from Dagenham and that dodgy bloke with the big bag of watches? And there wasn't a single German on a sun lounger when we visited – all very confusing.
Mon-Fri 12pm-11pm, Sat 12pm-11.30pm, Sun 12pm-11pm
Jamon Serrano (tapas portion) £3.75, House wine £10.95

Nandos

The Light, The Headrow (0113) 242 8908

Ok, it's actually Portuguese, not Spanish or South American, but geography's never been our strong point and we didn't have room for another section anyway. Nandos'll dish up every bit of chicken you can think of, doused in their spicy peri-peri sauce and served with sides like coleslaw and corn on the cob. You have to pay at the counter before, rather than after, and the soft drinks and frozen yoghurt are self service. I guess it prevents the youth of today from doing a runner and gives them a taste of the service industry in one.

Mon-Thu 11am-11pm, Fri-Sat 11am-12am, Sun 11am-10.30pm
Chicken breast burger with a sideline £5.10, House wine £9.95

Viva Cuba

342 Kirkstall Road (0113) 275 0888

If you haven't found this magnificent tapas place yet, then you're obviously not serious about getting a good meal inside you. Small and intimate, they've got a whole new floor planned for 2005, meaning they can share the wealth with all the more of us – not that they're ever short of takers. Authentic Cuban artwork and knick-knacks on the wall, weekly live music and as much Havana rum as you can drink – there's atmosphere in bucketloads and the friendliest management around. Menu-wise you'll have problems deciding between it all, but with plentiful portions served up in cute terracotta pots, you'll be back to try the rest of the menu in a flash.

Mon-Thu 6pm-11pm, Fri-Sat 5pm-11pm, Sun 5pm-10.30pm (opening hours soon to be extended, call for details)
Pimentos con queso de crema £2.95, House wine £11

Jino's Thai Café

46a Otley Road (0113) 278 8088

It's a source of constant frustration to us that we've yet to come across a Thai restaurant called "Thai a Yellow Ribbon round the Old Oak Tree". And as this one opened in Headingley last year – just a stone's throw from the Original Oak pub – it's got some

explaining to do. But there's hope yet, for from humble beginnings this growing business has already expanded into the shop next-door. Who knows, before long it may have even completely surrounded the Oak leaving it with no option other than to change its name.

Tue-Sun 5pm-10pm
Thai green chicken curry £6.30, BYO

Sala Thai

Oakbank, 13-17 Shaw Lane
(0113) 278 8400

A 'sala' is a traditional roadside resting place where weary travellers can shelter and be refreshed before continuing their journey, and in that respect Sala Thai is well named. Set in a huge country house, complete with its own curved driveway, the traditionally attired waitresses will have you feeling like Yul Brynner in the 'King and I'. Indeed, Thai cuisine owes its uniqueness to self-rule and the fact that it's the only country in South East Asia which hasn't been colonized. Just check out the desserts to see what we mean – banana in coconut milk, you won't find that in your local Safeway. Delicate palettes may be surprised by the chilli factor – but we reckon it's all good taste bud training.

Mon-Sat 6pm-11pm
Thai roast duck in a spiced curry sauce with £7.50, House wine £8.50

Thai Edge

7 Calverley Street (0113) 243 6333

Budget travellers are always popping off to Bangkok for a summer of dirt cheap beer and street stall cuisine. Funny then, that you can live off a fiver a day there but for a Thai meal here you'll shell out the best part of

£40. Ok, so the waitresses wear traditional dress, and there's no crippling humidity, deadly diarrhoea or language barrier to deal with, but for dinner a deux from 'the land of smiles' we were lucky if the waitress cracked a grimace, let alone a full-on beam. Thank heaven for the Zen-like interior and frankly mouth-watering food.
Sun-Thu 5.30pm-11pm,
Fri-Sat 5.30pm-12am
Green curry £10.80, House wine £9.90

Other/Fusion

Arts Café, Bar & Restaurant
42 Call Lane (0113) 243 8243

10 years old and still making sure that no-one else gets a look-in, Arts continues to make sure its loyal customers are filled with good food, good conversation and feasting their eyes on fab local artwork. As friendly and relaxed as you could possibly hope for, its café stance during the day provides the perfect setting for a coffee and lunch plate, and come the evening, the a la carte food and extensive drinks menu won't fail to hook you in and keep you content for the whole night. Top-quality service, an impossibly high standard of food, and a cosy, creative atmosphere earn it a whole sheet of gold stars.
Mon-Sat 12pm-11pm, Sun 10am-10.30pm
Duo of sea bass and red mullet with
Mediterranean vegetables, asparagus and
pak choi £12.50, House wine £11.95

Baby Cream
153/155 The Headrow 08000 277 171

Atop the funky bar nestling seductively on the Headrow lies Baby Cream's elegant restaurant complete with chandeliers, tall windows and a Louis XIV-comes-to-Leeds kinda vibe. After getting warmed up in the sensual downstairs bar, head upstairs to sample their designed-to-be-shared menu, based on an updated 70s fondue style. With some dishes being cooked at the table and others requiring a bit of tearing and sharing, there's plenty of scope for intimate tete a tete dining, and portions big enough for a third guest if you're feeling crazy. Champagne cocktails, liqueurs and cigars on the drinks menu add extra class to an already decadent dining experience. See Bars too.
Lunch: Mon-Sun 12pm-2.45pm, Dinner:
Sun-Thu 6pm-10pm, Fri-Sat 6pm-12am
Soul seafood fondue (between 2-3)
£10.95, House wine £13.50

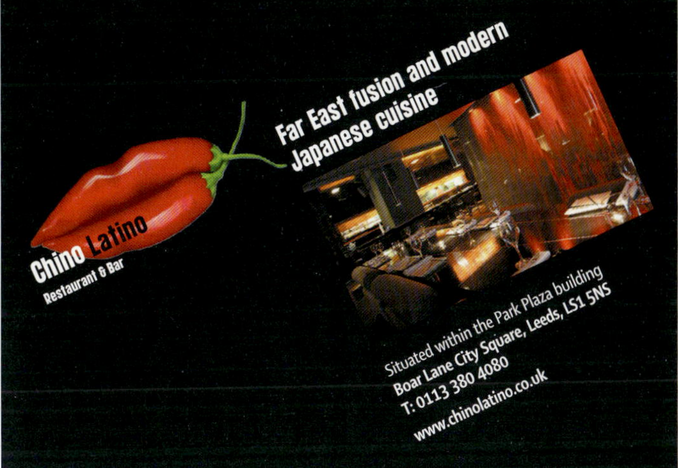

Brasserie Forty 4

42-44 The Calls (0113) 234 3232

This large brasserie occupies a former grain store and as a waterfront development on the prestigious Calls it considers itself far too good for the English language; thus the name 'forty 4' and its numerical equivalent are combined in a strange attempt at style. The food, view and atmosphere force us to forgive the name thing, though. Its target audience is defined by the fact they have a pre-opera dinner and business lunch deals, but it's well worth checking out even if you're not in the mood for closing a deal or checking out Wagner's Ring.

Mon-Fri 12pm-2pm/6pm-10.30pm,
Sat 6pm-11pm
Lunch/early dinner special: two courses
£12.50, third course supplement £3.50
Organic salmon £13.50, Wine from £12.20

Chino Latino

Park Plaza, City Square (0113) 380 4000

Guests of the Park Plaza hotel should be rubbing their hands in glee to have such a top class restaurant experience as part of their visit, but luckily non-residents can get in on the action too. A unique blend of Far Eastern fusion and modern Japanese cuisine expertly prepared by amongst others, an award-winning ex-Nobu head chef, the menu encapsulates essences of China, South East Asia, Thailand and Japan. There's nowhere else in the city offering anything like it. The cool, dark minimalist surroundings add to the buzzing atmosphere of the place, and with an impressive selection of bottled largers, wines, cocktails and Japanese sake, you'll want to kick back and relax long after your plates have been cleared.

Mon-Fri 7am-11am/12.30pm-

2.30pm/6.30pm-10.15pm
Sat 7am-11am/6.30pm-10.15pm,
Sun 8am-12am
Slow cooked spare ribs with sweet potato
£16, House wine £13

Citrus

13a North Lane (0113) 274 9002

A fantastic mid-way point between an intimate café and a posh eaterie, Citrus is a bright and airy café by day and suave minimalist eatery come the evening. The day menu boasts cold sandwiches and melts, salads, pasta and lighter meals, with the breakfasts being a massive draw for Headingley-ites, whether they be students, workers or a rare breed of native. Come the evening, things get a bit more upmarket with lowered lighting and a menu filled with a fusion of different flavours from exotic salads to modern British classics, but all great value for money. Head upstairs when you've savoured the flavours and shoot some pool to burn off all that fine food.

Day menu: Mon-Sun 9am-4.30pm,
Evening menu: Mon-Sun 4.30pm-10pm
Bar: Mon-Sun 12pm-11.30pm
Pan-fried escallop of pork loin with
Austrian ham wafer and marsala wine
sauce £9.95, House wine £8.95

Strawberry Fields

159 Woodhouse Lane (0113) 243 1515

They made a bar with a Beatles theme and decided to do some food, so we put their creation in the restaurant section. Then they started selling cheap absinthe and we wondered why the leprechauns kept telling us to burn down The Fenton all of a sudden. This place is really too small to guarantee a table when the evening drinkers come in, and there's probably nothing on the mainly vegetarian menu that you couldn't make at home anyway, but it's ideal for a budget lunch on the long walk from town to studentsville.

Mon-Fri 12pm-2pm/6pm-11pm,
Sat 6pm-11pm
Pizza and salad £3.99, House wine £7.99

The Wardrobe

6 St Peter's Buildings, St Peter's Square (0113) 383 8800

However fussy your taste buds or elastic your stomach, The Wardrobe can fix any culinary fantasy. Fill your face with a bumper brekkie after a hard night's partying, catch up with mates over a leisurely salad, soup or sandwich at lunchtime, or indulge in a spot of romancin' come nightfall with a few choice of meals from their a la carte menu of contemporary cuisine. A pre-theatre menu caters for the crowd stopping off for fuel before catching a play at the WYP next door,

and for those looking forward to evening propping up the bar, the extensive tapas menu is great for a satisfying feed.

Brunch: Mon-Sun 9am-3pm
Pre theatre: Mon-Sun 5pm-7 pm
A la carte: Mon-Sun 7pm-10pm
Pan-fried duck breast, served on a bed of cream cabbage and pancetta £11,
House wine £10
Pre-theatre menu: two course £13,
three course £15
Set menu (8 and over): 2 courses £16
Tapas: 3 for £6/6 for £10
Caters for most dietary requirements

Wetherspoon's

Leeds City Station, City Square
(0113) 247 1676
Stick Or Twist, Merrion Street
(0113) 234 9748
Beckett's Bank, 28-30 Park Row
(0113) 394 5900

There's a distinct lack of places in the city where you can get some decent pub grub without having to sacrifice a big wadge of cash for the privelege. Wetherspoon's might not be the most glamourous of eateries, but you can't argue with the value-for-money menu of burgers, panninis, wraps, sandwiches, pastas, jacket spuds and range of main meals and steaks. Beer-wise they're trying to introduce some more interesting beers to the drinks menu, so once you've polished off your loaded nachos, it makes sense to stay for a couple before you attempt to tackle the mean shopping crowds of Leeds – scary.

Food served from open 'til one hour before closing (see Bars section for more details)
Peri-peri chicken wrap £3.99,
House wine £5.99

Hansa Gujarati

72-74 North Street (0113) 244 4408

This homely Gujarat restaurant has been around almost as long as Joss Stone (17 years to be exact), but unlike Ms Stone it's staying firmly put (and not sodding off to America to adopt a fake NYC twang and hang out with Tom Cruise). Offering traditional Indian vegetarian dishes, the thali complete meal is recommended to experience the region's full flavours. And if you can fit anything else in, there's a tasty selection of lassis, vegan deserts and chai tea. Suitably inspired? Look out for special events like the cookery demonstrations and start turning your kitchen into a regular taste of the exotic.

Mon-Fri 5pm-10.30pm, Sat 5pm-11pm,
Sun (buffet lunch) 12pm-2.30pm
Early bird menu: Mon-Fri 5pm-6pm
Methi bateta (potato curry with fenugreek herbs) £5.25, House wine £10.50

bars

brb

37 Call Lane (0113) 243 0315

There are so many sofas in this place with so many people talking so much bollocks that it's almost like appearing on GMTV. But that's the price you have to pay when your bar's known as one of the coolest in Leeds. The best thing to do is make the most of the GMTV similarities by settling down to ogle all the weather girls on show, then simply kicking back to the laid-back tunes. The popular Tuesday 241 pizza deal still exists and the upstairs bar cum Swedish sauna cum club is a bevy of designer-clad beauties come the weekend – the perfect place for practising Lorraine Kelly's chat-up tips.

Sun-Wed 12pm-12am, Thu-Fri 12pm-1am, Sat 12pm-2am
Food: 12pm-11pm/12am
Chilli chicken pizza £6.95, House wine £10

The Elbow Room

64 Call Lane (0113) 245 7011

Call Lane's always been a prime spot for drinking, thanks largely to this pool hall cum funky bar. The lung-bustin' flight of

stairs might prove a chore for some, but once inside, your physical exertion will be rewarded with a plethora of pool tables, TV screens and a fine selection of burgers and beers to fill that hole that's been bothering you since lunch. Thankfully the pool tables mostly occupy an upstairs level, so you can enjoy a beverage in peace in the booth-style seats below without getting a cue in the eye every five minutes. DJs bring their record boxes along come the evening and show the decks who's boss, making it a buzzing spot for evening entertainment whether you're a pool shark, or more of a guppy where cue skills are concerned.

Mon-Thu 12pm-2am, Fri-Sat 12pm-3am, Sun 12pm-12am
Food: Mon-Sun 12pm-10pm
Lamb burger and fries £6.95,
House wine £8.50

Hakuna Matata
Swinegate (0113) 243 3586

Oh yeah? What sort of a name is Hakuna Matata, then? Not that it matters to all the trendy types who drink in here at lunchtime, because they're probably all called Piers, Marcus or Siobhan – except for the moments when they're known simply as 'wanker', of course. Walt Disney fans will naturally know that Hakuna Matata is an Elton John composition from the Lion King movie, but some might like to see one of his earlier works lauded here instead – 'Saturday Night's Alright For Fighting' would probably get a few nominations from the Ben Sherman set.

Mon-Sat 12pm-2am
Food: Mon-Thu 12pm-2pm/6pm-10pm,
Fri 12pm-2pm, Sat all day
Beef wrap £7.95, House wine £11.75

NORMAN
CLOSER THAN GOA
RESTAURANT BAR 36 CALL LANE LEEDS
01132 34 39 88

Milo

10 Call Lane (0113) 245 7101

Milo is strangely positioned between a fish and chip shop and a tattoo parlour, and that, unfortunately, is its major problem. All the larger venues have all been bought out by imagination-free chains like Yates's, leaving the decent bars with a bit of character hidden away from view. And so it is with Milo's, which is a bit on the small side, but if you can get in early enough to grab a table then it's an intimately-lit, funky little number to suit all tastes. And, of course, it's a belting place for copping off with fat birds who have 'I love chips' tattooed on their arses.

Tue-Thu 5pm-late, Fri 5pm-2am,
Sat 1pm-2am, closed Sun-Mon
Food: Sat 1pm-7pm
Club sandwich £2.96, House wine £9.95

Mook

Hirsts Yard (0113) 245 9967

You know us – salt of the earth types who like to 'keep it real' over pie and peas and a pint of bitter. But as much as we loved the gritty reality of The Whip, its site's successor, Mook, is much more sparkly and far less scary. Perfect for strutting around like you're worth it, this hidden away bar has a décor and clientele sprung straight from the pages of *Wallpaper. And if you were ever in doubt how a pint of lager could be stylish, just order a drink here – all sleek frothy loveliness served against a beautifully backlit bar. The extensive cocktail list should have something to match your outfit, but our money's always been on their trademark mookinis – which slip down as easily as a fat kid on a slide. With a soundtrack of laid-back beats and an exotic menu of finger food, it

may not be traditional Yorkshire, but all that bitter used to give us indigestion anyway.

Sun-Thu 4pm-12am/1am,
Fri-Sat 12pm-2am
Food: Mon-Sun 4pm-8pm
Fish finger sandwich £4, House wine £8.50

Norman

36 Call Lane (0113) 234 3988

A staple of the Leeds bar scene for so long now, but even the prettiest girls need to get a haircut every now and again if you know what we're saying. Out go the red seats and quirky décor, and in come white chairs, tan leather seating and expensive-looking chandeliers hanging seductively from the ceiling. Now more sleek and sophisticated than funky and retro, they've thankfully kept all of their best touches, from the beers and cocktails to the rice and noodle menu, selection of dim sum and cracking beer and meal deal for a fiver. Still packed as always, and tantalizingly displaying itself to the serfs on the outside through its impressive glass frontage, Norman's still as stormin' as ever.

Mon-Sat 12pm-2am, Sun 12pm-12am
Food: Mon-Sun 12pm-7.30pm
Singapore noodles £6.25, Dim sum from
£2.95, House wine £11

Oporto

31-33 Call Lane (0113) 243 4008
Being Oporto must be quite a stressful occupation, what with all those other cool bars plonking themselves in the same vicinity trying to nick its customers. Norman's

spruced himself up a bit and Jake's opened his bar and grill next door, but Oporto always makes sure he cleans behind his ears and has all the best drinks on offer like a good host should. A tapas-style menu of smaller dishes in the restaurant section makes it an excellent place for a lunchtime feed at lunch, but make sure you time your visit in the evening to make the most of the buzzing vibe and top-notch DJs. One of Call Lane's coolest, but not in the wanky or pretentious sense.
Mon-Sat 12pm-2am, Sun 1pm-12.30am
Food: Mon-Sun approx. 5pm-10pm
Tapas style menu from £3-£8
House wine £11.50

Reclaim

Calls Grill, 38 The Calls (0113) 245 3870
It's all about the wood. But before you call up 'Points Of View' to complain about our adult content, know that the wood at this intimate bar underneath The Calls Grill has been reclaimed from the dockside. If you're early for your table, or just like the environmentally-sound furnishing policy, this is the spot for pre-dinner drinks amidst grainy varnished tables and retro lighting. The food is as accomplished as the restaurant upstairs and come the summer you can enjoy your drink overlooking the dock. Aye aye c'ptain.
Mon-Sat 12pm-late, Sun 12pm-10.30pm
Food: Tue-Sat 12pm-3pm
Tomato and mozzarella sandwich £4.25,
House wine £11

Revolution

48 Call Lane (0113) 243 2778
Not everyone can appreciate the subtle oakiness of a fine chardonnay, or the perfect balance of hops and barley in a pint of the black stuff. In fact, some people never even acquire a taste for the booze, despite their love of its drunk-making properties. For those who like their poison to taste of

cordial, Revolution is the king of flavoured vodka. There are fruity ones, chocolate ones, minty ones, and ones that your friends will tell you are vanilla but are actually the painful chilli one that has a chemical peel-effect on the tongue. Get them back by pretending your mouth isn't in meltdown and bopping along to the DJ beats, or quench that thirst with one of the tasty cocktail pitchers – we

recommend the Russian Fruit Salad, with strawberry, raspberry and peach flavoured vodka. Mmmmm... tastes like candy.

Mon-Sat 12pm-2am, Sun 1pm-12.30am
Food: Mon-Sun 12pm-6pm
Steak baguette £5.50, House wine £9.50,
Vodka shots from £1.50

Townhouse

Assembly Street (0113) 219 4006

This is possibly Leeds' most popular venue at the moment, especially on club nights when all three floors are rammed to the teeth with excitable revellers dressed in their Friday night best. The ground level has a bar area with comfy seating and a café-style menu during daylight hours, while the third level is an out-and-out club, packed full of dressed-up beauties who count themselves luckily to be sipping on cocktails in the warm rather than freezing their toes off in the always massive queues. DJs keep the place interesting with a playlist of smooth tunes and eclectic grooves, and thanks to the three-floored format, you'll get a trio of

different parties for the price of one. Always packed full of people and never lacking in atmosphere, it's been at the top of Leeds' bar list for years now – and with good reason.

Mon-Sat 12pm-2am
Food: Mon-Sat 12pm-close
Paninis £2.95, House wine £13

The Wardrobe

6 St Peter's Buildings, St Peter's Square (0113) 383 8800

Laid-back, stylish and a solid front runner on Leeds' bar scene, The Wardrobe will see you right any night of the week, whatever party mood you happen to be in. Lubricate your night with their impressive range of cocktails, have a boogie to the live bands that feature in the upstairs café bar most nights of the week, or head downstairs for an all-singing, all-dancing, soul-tastic club night.

Casually chic, it's a fab place to while away a Saturday afternoon with a few coffees, and with a restaurant and club added on to the place, you'll struggle to drag yourself away come the evening. Undoubtedly one of Leeds' best.

Mon-Fri 9am-1am, Sat 12pm-1am,
Sun closed
Food: Mon-Sun 12pm-3pm/5pm-10pm
Tapas 3 for £6/6 for £10, House wine £10

Baby Cream

153-155 The Headrow 08000 277 171

Now this is more like it – it's been a while since we've had a bar to get properly excited about, and this one looks set to leap to the top of the Leeds' best bar lists without even breaking into a sweat. All bare wood and minimalist décor with the odd decadent twist, its location on the Headrow makes it a peach of a spot. Following on from the disgustingly successful Baby Cream in Liverpool, the Leeds branch has a lot to live up to, but with an affiliation to super-club brand Cream, it shouldn't prove too hard. Food-wise there's a classy and diverse menu of salads, platters, bowl food, grills and snacks, which are best washed down with one of their range of cocktails. Sumptuous, atmospheric and very, very classy, other bars will have to kick themselves up the backside to compete. See Restaurants too.

Mon-Sat 12pm-2am (closes at the manager's discretion, depending on custom),
Sun 12pm-12am
Food: Café menu served all day, full menu available in the restaurant
Chorizo chicken tortilla £5.95,
House wine £13.50

Bar Pacific

Swan Street (0113) 244 9130

Hidden away in an alleyway between Briggate and Lands Lane, Pacific's a fine venue for outdoor drinking that's lapped up by skiving office workers and lunching shoppers alike. It's always rammed when there's a show on at City Varieties, but also demands a look when on city centre drinking missions – the acoustic gigs on Thursday night offer a plausible excuse for midweek boozy action. Sunday is given over to chillout sessions on the venue's big sofas with all day breakfasts and Sunday lunch on the menu. There's also an 'Open Dex' policy which means the technics are available to anyone who feels like spinning some tunes.

Mon-Thu 12pm-11pm, Fri-Sat 12pm-1am,
Sun 12pm-6pm
Food: Mon-Fri 12pm-7pm,
Sat-Sun 12pm-5pm
Chicken breast with bacon and mustard sauce £6.50, House wine £7

Bar Risa

The Cube, Albion Street (0113) 247 1759

You've been drinking since seven and now it's nearly twelve. Your body's saying bed but as you make your wobbly way to the bus stop, the neon lights of Bar Risa start winking at you. Yes it's just another shiny city centre bar, but once the comedy's finished at Jongleurs next door you know that a couple of hundred tipsy punters will start mingling with Risa's already bustling clientele. So that's two venue's worth of tipsy totty to discover. What if one of those people is the man/woman of your dreams? So you wave goodbye to the no. 96 and pop in for a quick look around/one last drink/a

shimmy to Fat Man Scoop. Don't blame us if you come to on the pavement at 3am with a headache the size of West Yorkshire.

Mon-Sat 12pm-2am, Sun 12pm-12.30am
Food: Mon-Sun 12pm-6pm
Bangers & mash £5.50, House wine £11.50

Chino Latino

Park Plaza, City Square (0113) 380 4000

Sleek and stylish, the UK's second Chino Latino venture boasts a stunning restaurant and impressive cocktail bar, as well as occupying one of the peachiest spots in the city centre, below the swanky Park Plaza Hotel. The Far Eastern fusion and modern Japanese cuisine has to be its biggest draw, but the bar menu and stunning interior make it a great place for enjoying a drink (or four...) whether you're gagging for a bite to eat or not. The massive cocktail list includes rum, tequila and champagne based mixes, and there's a selection of sake choices for those game enough to try something new. Bottled lagers, wines from around the world and a range of Cuban cigars make sure there's always something tasty to get your lips around.

Mon-Sat 5pm-1am/2am
For food hours see Restaurants
Scallop sui mai £9, House wines from £13

Fab Café

46 Woodhouse Lane (0113) 244 9009

In a league of its own where style and concept are concerned, and one of those unique places where failing to have a good night is just not an option, nigh on actually impossible. Centred around cult television and movies, expect daleks, a model of the Star Ship Enterprise hanging from the ceiling and a massive collection of memorabilia that'll get you searching for your old Blue Peter annuals when you next visit your parents. Music is of the indie/classic pop ilk with everything from the Doves to Dee-lite whipping the crowd into a frenzied, dancing throng. Drinks are well priced, there are sweets and Pot Noodles on offer, it's like the dream home you never had as a nipper in the 80s.

Mon-Sat 4.30pm-2am, Sun 6pm-12.30am
Pot Noodles £1.50, House wine £1.70
(175ml)

Japanic

19 Queen Square (0113) 244 9550

Not all pairings are obvious – chocolate and cheese, Jordan and Peter Andre, and now East meets West Yorkshire at this pub cum karaoke bar. Settle in amidst the tea house décor for tapas-style Oriental cuisine – edamame, noodles, stir fries – or sip on sake in the dedicated karaoke lounge. If you're cautious of culture, ease yourself in gently with a pint of Stella and a bag of peanuts – we bet you'll be belting out Bananarama by the end of the evening.

Mon-Thu 12pm-1am, Fri-Sat 12pm-2am
Food: Mon-Fri 12pm-2am/6pm-10pm,
Sat 12pm-3pm/6pm-10pm
Beef yaki udon £3, House wine £3

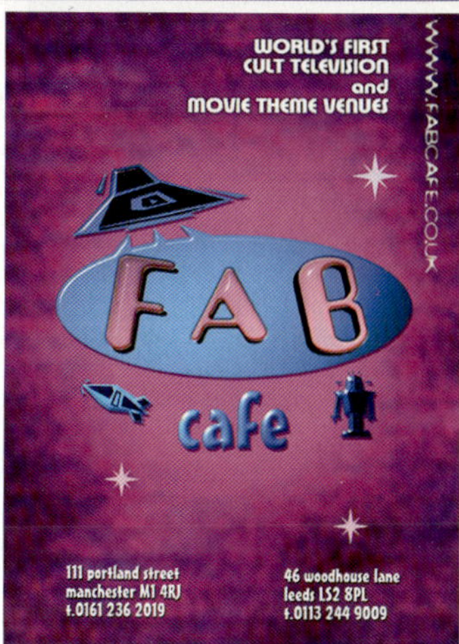

Life Bar

44-48 The Headrow (0113) 245 2575

Captain Kirk: "I'm picking up a signal that says there's some sort of Life ahead, Spock."
Spock: "Captain, sensors indicate that there are four bars, one club, one lounge and one restaurant."
Kirk: "Sounds interesting. Try a tri-quarter scan and see what else you can pick up."
Spock: "It shows a large moon inhabited by strange people. Most of its surface is covered in liquid and the people all appear to be on an island, behaving in a primitive way."
Kirk. "Aha. It must be Thursday. That's the Full Moon student night from the people who brought you Vodka Island."
Spock: "Full moon on top of Vodka Island? Is that a good idea?"
Kirk: "Was it a good idea for me to record a cover of Pulp's Common People? Get a life

and dance, you blue-blooded Vulcan!"
Aside from the weekly student siege, Life is your typical swish city centre chain – leather sofas, subdued lighting and funky house till the early hours. We wouldn't exactly call it intelligent life, but who can discuss the physics of inter-galactic travel after three vodka martinis?
Mon 11am-2am, Tue-Wed 11am-11.30pm, Thu-Sat 11am-2am, Sun 12pm-12.30am
Food: Mon-Sun 11am-9.30pm
Pork fillets £8.50, House wine £9.95

Lounge

**St John's Centre, Merrion Street
(0113) 244 4234**

You may not be called Oz, Jeremy or Michael, but that doesn't mean you can't enjoy the world of fine wine. In fact, pop down to Lounge, snuggle up on a sofa and dive mouth-first into their extensive fermented grape juice selection. Visiting more locations than a Bond movie, you can buff up your knowledge and then get stuck into the predominantly English food menu. If you want to dine in style, there's an 80-cover restaurant upstairs, which is also available to hire, a heated terrace, and a beautiful paved garden for the summer.
*Mon-Fri 11am-11pm, Sat 11am-1am,
Sun 12pm-10.30pm*
*Food: Mon-Fri 12pm-4pm/5pm-9pm,
Sat 12pm-9pm, Sun 12pm-6pm*
*Steak in pepper sauce with chunky chips
£6, House wine £10*

Room

**Bond House, Bourse Courtyard, Boar
Lane (0113) 242 6161**
This swish city centre spot claims to have

a room to suit your every mood. So that means the à la carte restaurant when you're feeling rich and hungry, a late bar, Bedroom, when you're feeling awake and sexy, and an outside room (i.e. the courtyard) for when you, and the weather, are feeling bright and sunny. But generally the mood you'll need to be in when you visit this venue is louche and relaxed, as you'll be mingling with PR peeps and business types, as well as moneyed guests of the Marriott nearby. The music pays homage to jazz, funk, soul, and reggae, while both the wine and cocktail list are extensive. Speaking of which, that's something your credit limit will have to be if you fancy an intimate dinner a deux. The à la carte menu offers such exotic creations as chicken nuggets and chips, and salmon 'pot noodle' for a staggering £14 each. Now that's what I call inflation…
*Mon-Tue 11am-11pm, Wed-Thu 11am-
12am, Fri-Sat 11am-2am, Sun 11am-5pm*
*Food: Mon-Tue 11am-10pm, Wed-Sat
11am-11pm, Sun 11am-4pm*
Steak bourguignon £14, Wine from £13.25

Tiger Tiger

The Light (0113) 236 6999
Like some multi-tasking demon, the Tiger Tiger chain aims to be all things to all peo-

ple, and as long as your tastes aren't too eclectic you'll find something to spark your interest here. On their own the themed bars (Canadian Lodge, Arabian Kaz Bar, tiled terrace, sunken lounge) are more individual than the venue as a whole – which because of its location has become the after work crowd's stop-off of choice. If you can still squeeze into your LBD join the queues for the 5pm-7pm happy hour; but if suited types make you sick, go on the prowl elsewhere.

Mon-Sat Mon 12pm- 12am,
Tue-Sat 12pm-2am, Sun 12pm-12am
Food: As above
Chump of lamb £12.95,
House wine £10.95
Fri-Sat £5 after 10pm

Financial District

Baby Jupiter

11 York Place (0113) 242 1202

About 10 years ago some pikey journo decided Leeds was the new centre of hip and ever since its been besieged by students, loft apartments and big name house DJs with suitcases full of plinky plonky piano beats. But some people like their music made with actual instruments, as opposed to computer programmes, so it's left to little havens like this to keep the spirit of the old school strong. It may be teeny, and the walls reminiscent of an acid flashback, but the mixed bag of monthly events includes everything from classic punk and new wave, to boogaloo, northern soul, and Madchester revival, as well as the odd smattering of local acoustic talent. Described on its own website as a 'cosmic hideaway... friendly faces,

real music and an atmosphere that's out there... somewhere', we couldn't have said it better ourselves.

Mon-Fri 12pm-11.30pm,
Sat 7pm-11.30pm
Food: Mon-Fri 12pm-2.30pm
Paella & bread £5.95, House wine £10.50

Firefly

21 Park Row (0113) 243 1122

A trendy bar that does food as well and a welcome relief to the otherwise stereotyped food choices in the city's financial district. The menu covers a lot of ground – seafood, game, poultry, a brunch menu – and gets away with it all rather well. The bar with its smart leather décor is ideal for reclining in after the grub's been shovelled down and it makes a perfect place for the slick Ricks and suave Marvs of this world to show off their flashy credit cards.

A la carte: Mon-Sat 12pm-11pm,
Sun 12pm-10.30pm
Fixed price menu: 2 courses for £10, 3 courses for £12.95 (Mon-Thu 12pm-11pm, Fri-Sat 12pm-7pm)
Brunch menu: Sun 12pm-6pm
Rump of lamb with aubergine and courgette gratin, potato fondant and sauce tapenade £13.95, House wine £12.50

Living Room

5-7 Greek Street 0870 44 22 720

It must be hard if you're rich in Yorkshire. I mean, it's not like London, where even breathing has a surcharge. So let's give a polite cricket clap to the Living Room – with its down-to-earth name and sky-high prices. £3 for a pint? A tenner for a chicken pie? And all within spitting distance of bargain brewery Wetherspoons! But then that's the thing, all your extra pennies have been spent making this place super swanky. Hold your martini glass at a jaunty angle in the main bar, slink seductively through the late bar Mosquito, comment on the cuisine in the Dining Room restaurant, or look all superior in The Study (a non-fee private members bar with a pool table). Even the music policy's suitably stylish – a mix of soul, pop, blues and boogie. God we hate it when we have to say "you get what you pay for", but in this case, it's true.

Mon-Tue 10am-12am, Wed-Thu 10am-1am, Fri-Sat 10am-2am, Sun 11am-12am
Food: Mon-Sun 12pm-12am
Chicken pie with mash £9.95,
House wine £10.75

Prohibition

Greek Street (0113) 224 0005

Prohibition by name, prohibition by nature. But before you whip that hip flask out of your pocket, know that it at least sells alcohol. It's just that all other types of fun seem right off the menu. We saw no dancing girls, no illegal gambling – hell, we were lucky to see anyone mush up their lip gloss to break into a smile. And as for the door staff – well let's just say they all seem to have undergone the same humour-bypass operation.

Still, there's plenty of seats to sit and sulk on and enough to satisfy even the most cavernous of stomachs. And we particularly enjoyed the red and black décor – very Soviet secret service. Which brings us back to that lack of humour thing...

Mon-Wed 12pm-12am, Thu 12pm-1am,
Fri-Sat 12pm-2am, Sun 12pm-12am
Food: Mon-Sun 12pm-10pm
Philadelphia steak sandwich £7.95,
House wine £10.50

Quid Pro Quo

Yorkshire House, Greek Street (0113) 244 8888

Run-of-the-mill bar in a street full of suit establishments, this place puts itself about as a 'wine & ale bar'. Of course, this being the Financial Sector it has to have a name that combines images of cash, professionalism and, er... Status Quo, which is why it's always full of old guys with suits and ponytails planning comeback albums and tours. But at least it's not half as pretentious as a lot of the places that surround it.

Mon-Wed 12pm-11pm,
Thu-Sat 12pm -2am, Sun closed
Food: Mon-Sun 12pm-8pm
Homemade burgers £5,
House wine £10.50

Millennium Square

Bourbon

43-51 Cookridge Street (0113) 244 1703

Highly-rated Bourbon is – surprise, surprise – student orientated and hires top DJs to thrash out the vinyl 'til stupid o'clock. All dark wood, leather sofas and artwork on the walls that make the nearby Leeds Met art students jitter with envy, its reputation has been riding strong for years now – largely thanks to the range of drinks offers and meal deals which make it a very popular choice with its target demographic from just up the hill. Popular with the after work crowd too, its imposing red frontage has the power to draw in even the stuffiest of office workers and give them a good night, and the three-sided bar makes for excellent across-bar winking opportunities. Just be careful who you stand opposite though, you know what office types are like after a few beers....

Mon-Thu 12pm-12am, Fri-Sat 12pm-2am, Sun 6pm-10.30pm
Food: Mon-Fri 12pm-6pm
Cous cous with lime roasted peppers £4.25, House wine £10

BOURBON

Owned by a former Leeds Student and run by Leeds students for Leeds students.

Jack Daniels is a registered trade mark of Jack Daniels

Qube

Millennium Square (0113) 234 3777
Aaah, Millennium Square – a vision of concrete slabs and windswept shrubbery. Just the thing to herald this fair city into the 21st century. Good thing then there's a whopping great bar on hand, to toast whichever clever clogs created such a vision of beauty. A handy stop off between The Headrow bars and the trio of Creation, Baja and Bourbon, Qube sees a steady flow of human traffic. Despite this, the atmosphere isn't exciting enough to spend a whole night here. The saving grace is the massive outdoor terrace, which is perfect for drinking the day away on come the summer.
Mon-Sun 11am-2am
Food: Mon-Sun 11am-17pm
Burger £5, House wine £9.75

chilled, intimate feel. Weekends see DJs adding to the fray with chilled hip hop and RnB on Friday and a funky, soulful selection on Saturday, and they also have facilities for people to play their own CDs, MP3s or iPod playlists (ask at the bar for details) should you be the next Gilles Petersen. A stunning array of drinks means you'll have to stay for the long haul, and with a stock list including 64 spirits and the best brands of each variety, it's bound to be a very good night.
Sun-Thu 6pm-1am, Fri-Sat 6pm-2am
No food, House wine £10.50

Northern Quarter

Mamylé

70-72 New Briggate 07821 415 050
Leeds' newest bar baby, Mamylé adds to the already classy selection in the Northern Quarter with its imposing frontage and

Mojo

18 Merrion Street (0113) 244 6387
For some reason this dingy shack down a Bronx-style alleyway is frequented by the trendiest people in Leeds – and Chris Moyles – which gives it its reputation for being the city's best bar. But you wouldn't think it when you walk in. There's a converted living room with a few seats and a long bar situated only on the one floor – simple but

effective. It's always rammed too, making the chances of finding a seat near impossible. But there's a great atmosphere, a strict music policy (guaranteeing a quality soundtrack of classic indie and rock), and the location makes sure that the rabble of town's eager pissed-up puppies usually bypass it entirely. It's the sort of place you can't just visit once. They do the best cocktails too – pricey, but devilish.

Mon-Thu 5pm-1am, Fri-Sat 5pm-2am,
Sun 5pm-12.30am
No food, House wine £8.50

North Bar

24 New Briggate (0113) 242 4540

Too many people stumble through life in a monotonous blur of responsibility and routine, but it doesn't have to be like this... Despite sounding like a flat cap and whippet place, North is actually a tiny tour of Europe. Run by people who take their drinking seriously, there's a selection of over 70 beers in stock at any one time – encompassing brews from Germany, Belgium, Holland, Mexico, Thailand, Australia and Sri Lanka. Add to this a regularly changing hand-pulled English ale, and shelves straining with rums, bourbons, wines and cigars, and you could turn tipsy by osmosis alone. Good job that also do a fine line in tapas and finger food. Line your stomach whilst you appreciate the local artwork on the walls, before getting back to the boozing with a friendly and eclectic crowd.

Mon-Tue 12pm-1am, Sun 12pm-2am,
Sun 12pm-10.30pm
Food: As above
Sandwiches and platters from £1.50-£6,
House wine £9.95

MAMYLÉ
BAR

70 – 72 New Briggate
Leeds LS1 6NU

www.mamyle.com

The Reform

12/14 Merrion Street (0113) 244 4080

One of the places in the city that's seen the most changes over the years, what used to be minimalist hangout Isis has now transformed itself into a stylish bar with a vintage feel thanks to bold blocks of intricate wallpaper and decadent leather armchairs. Its striking red exterior will draw your eyes (if not your belly) from the curry place next door, though Mojo is always an industrial strength magnet to cool folk, so leave your studded belt at home. But bless this bar with your drinking time and wallet full of cash and you'll have a top notch night full of DJs, continental beers and as many expertly-mixed cocktails as your mouth/stomach will hold. Keep your eyes peeled for a new cult film room due to open in mid-2005 too.

Mon-Sat 5pm-2am (due to open on

Sundays soon – call for details)
Mon-Sat 5pm-8pm (after if quiet)
Paninis £2.50, House wine £11.90

Sandinista!

5 Cross Belgrave Street (0113) 305 0372

With flags blowing bravely in the wind and a cheeky devil type character winking on the roof, Sandinista! refuses to be ignored, despite being located in one of the quieter bits of town. Its external bravado is more than justified though; inside you'll be greeted with wooden furniture, a huge array of

spirits and the occasional live band, giving it an authentic Latino cantina feel – more than appropriate seeing as it shares its name with a bunch of Nicaraguan revolutionaries. A menu of faithful cantina dishes and a range of tapas keep the eating crowd smiling, and with late nights all week, it's a top spot for party-loving insomniacs too.

Mon-Tue 12pm-12am,
Wed-Thu 12pm-1am, Fri-Sat 12pm-2am,
Sun 12pm-12.30am
Food: Mon-Thu 12pm-10pm,
Fri-Sun 12pm-9pm
Piccadillo £5.50, House wine £11

The Arc

19 Ash Road (0113) 275 2223

In true biblical fashion, pretty pairs of boys and girls flock to this two-floored glass palace to find shelter against Yorkshire's torrential weather conditions. But for every forty or so bright young things, you'll find a dirty old Noah – albeit a foot tappin' Status Quo lookalike who's swapped the flowing beard for a fetching mullet. His piss-poor chat up lines have a herding effect – making the young fillies move as far from him as possible, before pairing up with the first specimen they can find under 40. Should evolution need a helping hand, the two bars serve up a staggering selection of cocktails to oil the wheels of love, and the reasonably priced restaurant makes hunting and gathering for your new family a doddle.

Mon-Wed 11am-11pm,
Thu-Sat 11am-12pm, Sun 11am-10pm
Food: Mon-Sat 11am-10pm, Sun till 9pm
Tagliatelle £6.45, House wine £8.50

Arcadia

Arndale Centre, Otley Road
(0113) 274 5599

...Or to give it its full name, 'Arcadia Ale & Wine Bar'. This throwback to the 80s is a cross between a Hamburg beer haus and the sort of place depicted in that classic 'Only Fools and Horses' episode. But while its roots may lie in the decade that taste took a holiday from, its ethos is distinctly new-age. Stating its intentions as subtly as the four foot chalkboard outside allows, this is bar is strictly no-smoking – possibly a precurser to Britain following Dublin, Norway and the west coast of America with a public smoking ban. If that isn't enough to put you young rebels off, the clientele this attracts is mainly middle-aged Wilkinson shoppers, people who think they know 'a thing or two' about wine, and anyone whose doctor has scared them into the healthy life. As dull as that sounds.

Mon-Sun 11am-11pm, Sun 12pm-10.30pm
Food: Mon-Fri 12pm-2pm/6pm-8pm,
Sat 12pm-7pm, Sun 12pm-2.30pm
Spicy venison sausage with leek mash
£6.95, House wine £10.45

The Box

8 Otley Road (0113) 224 9266

The first thing that'll strike the regular pub-goer about The Box is the sheer size of the pool tables. These are proper bona-fide pool tables. Mind you, with plenty of place to stand round these giant baize creatures, it means plenty more people can see you're a shite player. So we'd suggest checking out the professionals on the numerous sports screens instead, or alternatively admire the jiggling buttocks on MTV. There are some pretty cheap lunch deals on offer, but if you want a drink to accompany that ass appreciation you'll find the age-old equation of leather(L) + chrome(Ch) = average cost of pint(ACP) + 50p, which consequently attracts some rather tedious mathematicians and the unpleasantly wealthy.

Mon-Fri 10am-11pm, Sat 10am-1am,
Sun 10am-12.30am
Food: 10am-8pm
Big breakfast £4.75, House wine £8.50

Trio

44 North Lane (0113) 203 6090

Following Arc's two-by-two example (two floors, two bars...), Trio goes one better and slaps another level on. Encompassing (from the top) a swanky lounge, restaurant, and basement bar, the overall look of leather sofas and blonde wood tramples all over the neighbouring takeaways and corner shops. The majority of the mayhem takes place downstairs though, in the subterranean bar. Slicked-up students sip on Singapore slings, and sample the exotic ales on offer – including Germany's Erdinger, Tsing Tao from China, and the Belgian Leffe. Should those potent brews go to you head, this dimly-lit den is the perfect place to slink on a sofa until its time to go home. Which will be by foot, by the way, as the bar prices won't leave you with enough cash for a taxi.

Mon-Sat 5pm-11pm, Sun 5pm-10.30pm
Food: Mon-Fri 12pm-3pm/6pm-11pm,
Sat-Sun 12pm-11pm
Wood-fired pizza £6.50, House wine £9.50

babycream

153 - 155 The Headrow Leeds LS1 5RB

0113 3804320

www.babycream.co.uk

Opening hours are Mon-Sat 11am-11pm and Sun 12pm-10.30pm, unless otherwise stated

Exchange Quarter

Aire
32 The Calls (0113) 203 1811

Not everyone can afford a swanky city centre apartment, but as long as you have a couple of quid in your pocket you can pull up a seat at this riverside pub, sit back and breathe in the fumes to your heart's content. Actually, that's just us being bitter – the wooden balcony here is a welcome relief from the bustle of town and has the added bonus of being opposite aforementioned posh pads – so if you're lucky you might see an upwardly mobile type getting undressed or something. Inside, it's a hotch-potch of leather sofas, bar bricks and patterned rugs, with some solid lunches and a friendly atmosphere. Kick back and relax – this is the closest you'll get to an address in The Calls...
Food: Mon-Sun 12pm-5.30pm

pubs

O'Neill's

Great George Street (0113) 244 0810
Ireland has a reputation for exports of varying calibre but, lest we forget, for every fun-filled Colin Farrell there's a tiresomely dull Bryan McFadden. Leeds has strong links with the Emerald Isle – with many thousands of its inhabitants having migrated here over the last 100 years or so – so it seems strange that O'Neill's is its only Celtic watering hole. Expect fair-priced pints, big screen sports and a gaggle or two of wooden puffins (although we wouldn't recommend the food). Now if only the office workers would piss off.
Mon-Thu 11.30am-11pm,
Fri-Sat 11.30am-12am,
Sun 12pm-10.30pm
Food: Sun-Thu 11.30am/12pm-9pm,
Fri-Sat 11.30am-7pm

Barracuda Bar

20 Woodhouse Lane (0113) 244 1212
The nearby McDonald's might be a better place to go if you're after a bite to eat, but South African-themed Barracuda does the job for sports fans looking for cheap booze and lots of tellies. Conveniently, drinks are just a quid apiece on Tuesdays – a big football night – and you'll never struggle to get a view of a screen. You might even be lucky enough to sit at one of the booths with a screen right next to your table, which is just what you need for the Crewe vs Tranmere game.
Mon-Wed 11am-11pm, Thu 11am-12am,
Fri-Sat 11am-2am, Sun 12pm-11pm
Food: Mon-Sat 11am-6pm, Sun 12pm-6pm

Walkabout

Cookridge Street (0113) 205 6500
Named after the cult 70s film featuring Jenny Agutter wandering starkers round the Aussie outback, this down under bar specialises in pulling in crowds for the big games of the rugby season. Typically heaving with flash-bonced Bruces in vests and flip-flops, and suspiciously bronze-tinted Sheilas showing plenty of coconuts and legs (i.e. giggly uni students). Sadly none of them, male or female, seem prepared to take off all their kit and go walkabout. Shame.
Mon 11am-11pm, Tue 11am-12am,
Thu 11am-1am, Wed/Fri-Sat 11am-2am
Food: Mon 11am-10pm, Tue 11am-11pm,
Wed/Fri-Sat 11am-1am, Thu 11am-12am,

Victoria Commercial Hotel

Great George Street (0113) 246 1386
If you were a tourist arriving in Yorkshire for the first time then this is the sort of pub you'd expect to come across. A traditional brewery pub with hanging baskets, polished brass, and stained glass, it adds weight to the archetypal old codger's argument that things aren't what they used to be. A lot of pubs like this tend to be a bit uncomfortable for young ravers but that's not the case here.

The atmosphere's warm and friendly whether you be a Stella swilling whipper-snapper or stout sipping grandma. Lovely.
Mon-Sat 11.30am-11pm, Sun closed
Food: Mon-Sat 12pm-7pm

City Centre

The Angel Inn
Angel Inn Yard (0113) 245 1428

Living up to its name, this heavenly pub has alighted upon Leeds city centre to spread joy and happiness to all those made weary by the city's identikit drinking houses. Peddling Sam Smith's superior brews, you can happily enjoy an evening's drinking and still get change from a tenner (obviously depending on how much you can stow away). Pull up a stool amidst the portraits and fireplace and let the band of wizened regulars tell you how this is what pubs used to be like before they got snapped up by wealthy conglomerates. One visit and you'll want to come back again and again. Shame then, that its position down a hidden alleyway means you'll spend the rest of the year wondering where it went to. Was it all just a dream...?
Food: Mon-Fri 12pm-3pm/5pm-7pm, Sat 12pm-7pm, Sun 12pm-2.30pm

Beckett's Bank
28-30 Park Row (0113) 394 5900

Yeah, yeah, it's a Wetherspoon's and we're risking a public flogging by sticking our neck out and bigging this place up, but sod it, we've always been the type of folk to be the shepherds rather than the sheep. A great spot for a quick burger and a pint during your lunch hour, their menu's consistently good value and there's always some kind of cheap offer on to entice you in. Believe it or not, even the CAMRA chaps are getting involved by working with the chain to bring in new, unusual and interesting beers from various brewers, big and small, to the uneducated masses. A handy city centre location makes it a sterling choice for a night out or a session during the day if you're in the area. Go on, take the plunge.
Mon-Sat 10am-11pm, Sun 10am-10.30pm
Food: Mon-Sun 10am-1hr before close

Edwards
Merrion Street (0113) 246 9297

It'd be harsh to judge Edwards against pubs that aren't cynically tacked onto shopping centres like giant, vomit-smelling barnacles, but here goes: Edwards is a haven for young professionals with no money in £35 Asda suits and predatory divorcees of all kinds, lured together by alcopops and a playlist that would make Noel Edmonds shudder. Those easily angered by such awfulness would do well to pop a Xanax before visiting, but saying that, unless you're conducting a field experiment on the mating rituals of the chronically hopeless you shouldn't have reason to even notice the place.
Mon-Thu 11am-11pm, Fri-Sat 11am-12am, Sun 12pm-10.30pm

Great food at
Wetherspoons

...Becketts Bank	28-30 Park Row, Leeds	0113 394 5900
...The Three Hulats	13 Harrogate Road, Chapel Allerton, Leeds	0113 262 0524
...Stick or Twist	The Podium Site, Merrion Way, Leeds	0113 234 9748
...Wetherspoons	Leeds City Railway Station, North Concourse	0113 247 1676

*Choose from a selected range. We monitor the presence of nuts in all of our products, however; we cannot guarantee that any items are free from traces of nuts. Subject to availability. Photography is for guidance only.

The Grove Inn

Back Row (0113) 243 9254

One of the last symbols of inner-city working class Holbeck, and it seems intent on standing its ground while its neighbours are knocked down or rebuilt for the benefit of potential office workers. A traditional pub of the highest quality, there's a constant stream of impressive live music. But before you start brushing up on you're A&R skills, the genres on offer are typified by the regular Friday folk night, which has been running for 30 years. One of our favourite pubs in Leeds.

Mon-Sat 12pm-11pm, Sun 12pm-10.30pm
Food: Mon-Fri 12pm-2pm, Sun 1pm-3pm

Joseph's Well

Hanover Walk (0113) 245 0875

Sadly there's no well in this pub, as it'd be a useful place to dump the more moth-ridden regulars. Still, it attracts a number of established bands as well as up-and-coming rock'n'roll cadets. Live music is its lifeblood but its late closing makes it popular with pub-goers who want just one more drink before whatever comes next. Indigestion probably.

Mon-Fri 12pm-12am, Sat 5pm-12am,
Sun 12pm-10.30pm
Food: Mon-Sun 12pm-2pm

Scarborough Hotel

Bishopgate Street (0113) 243 4590

Its proximity to the train station has meant that this city centre boozer used to be an old favourite with away fans before making their way towards Elland Road. And that in turn made it popular with Leeds United fans who wanted to get inside and kick their heads in. Add to that the meetings of Far

Right groups that went on here in the 1970s and you have more battle history than the British Museum. Things have changed since then though, and the pub's undergone a revamp in recent times which has even started tempting in students and city suits. Actually, that sounds like a potential fight's in the offing....

Food: Mon-Sat 11am-7pm, Sun 12pm-7pm

Stick or Twist

Merrion Street (0113) 234 9748

Located next to a casino, your reasons for drinking in here are probably somehow connected to its neighbour, whether it be the drowning of sorrows and counting of last pennies or the rare celebration of a big win (yeah, right). Clear your head of those pesky gambling voices for one minute though, and you'll notice the no frills menu of burgers, paninis and the like, and a selection of booze that includes proper real ales and everything (selected with the help of those CAMRA folk). They even won top prize in the 2004 Leeds In Bloom competition – now that's making an effort. Stay a while longer next time and give them some love back.

Mon-Sun 10am-11pm
Food: all day until one hour before closed

Wetherspoon's

Leeds City Station, City Square
(0113) 247 1676

We could get on our soapbox about the state of this country's rail system, but we'll just head to this handy train station boozer and talk about Abi Titmuss' lack of morals instead. Cheap, cheerful and always packed full of folk making friends with massive suitcases, come the summer the outside terrace area is the perfect vantage spot for taking in tearful goodbyes and enthusiastic welcomes from people foolish enough to forsake their own motorcar for a young person's railcard. A value-packed menu of burgers, sandwiches and litebites make for good train delay fodder.

Mon-Fri 7.30am-11pm, Sat 9am-11pm,
Sun 10am-10.30pm
Food: Mon-Sun 10am-1hr before closing

Whitelocks

Turks Head Yard (Off Briggate)
(0113) 245 3950

One of Leeds' hidden treasures, Whitelock's was founded on this site in the early 1700s and many of the building's best features are still in attendance. It's an old-fashioned, good food pub and a hearty lunch is on the cards if you choose to eat inside. Although close to the city's main shopping precinct there are usually some free tables, perhaps because it's another of those traditional Leeds pubs that cheekily hides itself down an alleyway.

Food: Mon-Sun 12pm-7pm

University Area

Dry Dock

Woodhouse Lane (0113) 203 1841

Drag an old barge half-a-mile from the nearest waterway and park it on a traffic island outside a university and you just know that students are going to drink in it. And that's the logic behind the Dry Dock, where students ply themselves with low cost liquor courtesy of their 'Yellow Card' deals and then sing bloody boat songs all the way back to their halls. Everyone else might consider giving it the red card.

Mon-Sat 12pm-1am, Sun 12pm-12am
Food: Mon-Sun 12pm-6pm

The Faversham

Springfield Mount (0113) 243 1481

Now run by the folk who have made the HiFi Club and Arts Café such runaway hits, out goes the tacky 'It's A Scream' style décor, and in comes a funky minimalist, retro look, complete with long lighted bar, leather sofas, mosaic tables and booth-style seating. Menu-wise, expect light bites at lunch and more substantial meals in the evening, and spectacular Sunday roasts, all complemented by a fruity cocktail menu and impressive range of beers and spirits. With a fantastic programme of nights and live music (see Clubs section), there's plenty to keep you interested, but a place of this quality needs to make little effort in that department. In the peaks and troughs that are the Faversham's history, this era is practically Mount Killamajaro.

Mon-Thu 12pm-2am, Fri-Sat 12pm-3am,
Sun 12pm-1am
Food: Mon-Sat 12pm-7.30pm,
Sun 12pm-6pm

The Fenton

Woodhouse Lane (0113) 245 3908

Just across the road from the old BBC building and home to an eclectic mix of students, lecturers and shiny happy meedja types. There's live music in the upstairs room at weekends but otherwise it's a rather humdrum northern boozer. Thursday night happy hours appeal to the university scruffs.

Fri-Sat 12pm-11pm, Sun 12pm-10.30pm
Food: Mon-Thu 11.30am-7pm,
Fri-Sat 12pm-4pm

The Library

229 Woodhouse Lane (0113) 244 0794

One third of the Otley Run Bermuda Triangle, in which the lightweights (or at least their wallet, phone, and shoes) begin to mysteriously go missing. Also one of the best places in the area for (non-Leeds United) football fans to criticise professional athletes while drinking beer and smoking. This is because, unlike the 'Horse and the Eldon, it's possible to see at least one of the televisions from anywhere in the building.

Food: Mon-Sun 12pm-5pm

The Pack Horse

208 Woodhouse Lane (0113) 245 3980

Ah, the dear old "Horse" may be of an age when the knacker's yard beckons, but pat her on the head from time to time and she'll happily reward you with a frothy pint of bitter and a smile from a busty rock chick barmaid or toothless local. It's also the regular pit-stop of Boy George's cousin, who can always be relied upon to mumble something about the Belfast shipyards and, no matter how many times he's seen you before, mention that he's 'By George's' cousin, and happily pose for pictures. Aside from this, there's a cosy pool room (mind the windows when you cue up), a legendary juke box and a new upstairs bit, which unfortunately doesn't share the charm of the floor below.

Food: Mon-Sat 12pm-7pm

Headingley/Hyde Park Area

Headingley Taps

North Lane (0113) 220 0931

Once a local pumping station, these days the taps in question manage the flow of ale, rather than the flow of bathwater to Mr and Mrs Higgins at 122. The Victorian architecture cuts a pretty imposing view on the landscape, but unless your neck prevents you from looking up, you still can't miss the giant car park out front. Doubling as a beer garden come summer, you can enjoy your pint amidst a host of Headingley residents' transport facilities – a must for any wannabe Jeremy Clarksons. Inside, it often seems unnaturally bright, but in our experience this only helps highlight unacceptable behaviour, leading to a well-behaved (if lively) crowd and a good view of the talent. Hearty meals are on offer, and for the more adventurous, Sunday night karaoke.

Food: Mon-Fri 11am-7pm,
Sat-Sun 11am-5.30pm

Hyde Park

Hyde Park Corner (0113) 274 5597

It's easy to see why the Hyde Park is so-called. The clientele could have been clean-cut Dr Jekylls before they went to the bar and downed that pint. And now? ... Blimey! Even the girls have got hairy hands and mutton-chop whiskers. It's absolutely overflowing with scruffy students and even scruffier locals who manage to turn ugliness into a spectator sport. Turn up and gawp at them by all means but don't expect to get a seat to watch the football. Don't bother waiting to get onto a pool table either unless you've got a few hours to spare. And don't bother sitting on the outside benches by the traffic lights either – the pollution alone could gas a small child in seconds. Fit bar maid, though.

Food: Mon-Fri 12pm-7pm,
Sat-Sun 12pm-5pm

Hyde Park Social Club

Hyde Park (0113) 293 0109

The influence of the sinister Mr Hyde is here again as student fans of the alternative/indie scene brainwash the mainstream LS6 community in their own backyard and turn them into zombies. This happy-clappy working class club is now full of hairy students and their local sidekicks who are into live music and stapling their faces.

Mon-Fri 3.30pm-11pm, Sat 2pm-11pm, Sun 2pm-10.30pm
No food

New Inn

68 Otley Road (0113) 224 9131

Part of a knot of pubs on Otley Road that owe their continuing existence to thirsty students. This modest little cottage has just the one bar and one pool table inside it but you can still buy 30 pints and stand outside with your 30 mates, talking bollocks and getting in the way of the elderly locals who are trying to do their shopping.

Food: Mon-Sun 12pm-2.30pm

The Original Oak

2 Otley Road (0113) 275 1322

The original and the best, The Oak sits with its partner in crime, The Skyrack, on either

side of Otley Road like the gateposts to Gin Lane. Inside their doors the wasters and slackers of the earth are all crammed together with a few non-students as well. Most seem to go on a yo-yo pub crawl from one to the other all day taking full advantage of one of the most overused pedestrian crossings in the country, and both are particularly busy on Headingley Stadium match days. In summer The Oak has a beautifully big beer garden, which is besieged as soon as the temperature rises above freezing. We love it.

Food: Mon-Fri 12pm-7pm, Sat 12pm-5pm, Sun 12pm-4pm

The Royal Park

Queens Road (0113) 275 7494

The Royal Park is a huge palace of a pub with about a million pool tables, a basement gig venue and a buzzing atmosphere. There's also a large congregation of clever dicks inside it who win all the pub quizzes. But, as is often the case, there's a brains-before-beauty policy at work, making this

boozer's regulars some of the ugliest fuckers to be found in this solar system. Put it on your "places to visit" list next to Tropical World and the Royal Armouries and give it a tour on a rainy day. Recommended for anthropology students who don't mind losing team quiz games.
Food: Mon-Fri 5pm-8pm,
Sat-Sun 12pm-4pm/5pm-8pm

The Skyrack

2 Otley Road (0113) 278 1519

Gareth Gates, Man United, and the Conservative Party are all evidence that coming second can doom you to a lifetime of hatred, ridicule, or at the very least public humiliation at the hands of Jordan. And by that logic Headingley's second favourite pub should be as unpopular as the aforementioned. However, thanks to the unstrenuous uni timetables and a licence that allows you to liver-pickle after the Oak has closed, this place is packed carpet to curtain with pie-eyed uni sports teams drinking themselves to an early grave. God bless the education system.
Mon-Tue 11am-11pm,
Wed-Sat 11am-12.30am,
Sun 12pm-12.30am
Food: Mon-Sun 12pm-7pm

Three Horseshoes

98 Otley Road (0113) 275 7222

Over the years the Three Horseshoes has been the source of many dreadful attempts at jokes about horses with three legs, but not anymore. The horseshoe, of course, is a symbol of good luck and with three of them on your side you can only be on to a winner with this popular pub. The chances are that if you visit this place you'll enjoy some bargain bar food, make some new friends and even score with one of the attractive young ladies behind the bar. On the other hand, you could drink far too much, wake up in a field, and then find out that the bird you've just shagged is really a three-legged horse. You make your own luck in this world, pal, but cheap beer pulls the students in from the nearby halls, so the odds are looking good.
Food: Mon-Fri 12pm-8pm, Sun 12pm-4pm

Woodies

104 Otley Road (0113) 278 4393

Positioned just a hoof away from the Three Horsehoes, this is more of a local than a student pub... unless it's the day a 20-strong group of gangsters and molls decide to embark on the Otley Run. A beer garden gives Woodies the edge on its neighbours on summer evenings, and a good jukebox and big screen provide all the entertainment you need – apart from jokes about three-legged horses that is.
Food: Mon-Sat 12pm-2pm

clubs

Atrium
6-9 Grand Arcade (0113) 242 6116

One of the most eclectic and diverse clubs in the city, the three-floored Atrium has an army of loyal fans who can't get enough of the basement nightclub, middle floor bar and top floor lounge. Weekends bring some sterling nights including nationally acclaimed RnB/salsa night 'Salsoul!' complete with salsa dance classes and dance shows. Saturdays bring 'Mardi Gras', a three-floored mix of funky beats and grooves and for those who fancy getting down to

the hard stuff, pole dancing classes on a Monday are a treat. Free admission during the week gets party fiends rejoicing into the night, and with DJs like Mr Scruff and Gilles Petersen bringing their record boxes, there's always plenty to keep serious DJ spotters interested. Not the biggest place in town, but its intimate atmosphere and funky vibe simply can't be beat.

Mon/Wed-Thu 9pm-2am, Tue 7.30pm-10.30pm (pole dancing classes)/10.30pm-2am, Fri 7.30pm-9.30pm (salsa classes)/10.30pm-3am, Sat 9pm-3am
Mon-Thu free, Fri-Sat £3-£5

Baja Beach Club

43a Woodhouse Lane (0113) 245 4088

Not many clubs manage to combine Sunday Night at the London Palladium with an amateur porn film and get away with it, but Baja seems to. On show most nights are male strippers, cocktail-spinners, bikini girls, and even showbizzy Abba performers. But the best acts are the piss-heads. Even the sturdiest Ben Sherman shirt wearers are happy to guzzle down lurid alcopops while doing that booty-dance that makes all but the hottest sexy mamas look like they're riding an imaginary horse. So you'd better butter your knees and thro-o-o-w your torso if you wanna pull in this bamboo-lined shag hut – and you'd better hope that the stupid plastic shark suspended from the ceiling isn't hiding a secret camera. Speaking of which, however pissed you are don't sign anything on your way out, or you could be the star of a documentary on 'today's shameful drinking generation'.

Mon/Wed/Thu 9pm-2am,
Tue 9.30pm-2.30am, Fri-Sat 8pm-2.30am,
Sun 9pm-1am
Free before 10pm/£3-£5 after

Bar Phono

16 The Merrion Centre (0113) 242 9222

Joe Strummer from the Clash once livened up this underground crypt by busking outside the door, and even though he's been dead for two years he'd still liven the place up if he did the same again. Bar Phono has outlived so many of its club scene competitors (its existence stretches back over three decades) but, just like the Merrion Shopping Centre that sits on its head, it's looking less and less attractive; and the goths, moths and rockers that have taken shelter in its bowels will soon have to face the daylight. Maybe someone should set up some form of outreach programme?

Wed 10pm-2am, Thu 10pm-2am,
Fri-Sat 9.30pm-2.30am, Sun 7pm-12am
Wed £2-£4, Thu-Fri £2-£3, Sat £1-£4,
Sun £10 (1 year's membership)

The Bassment

Wade Lane, Merrion Centre (0113) 245 0689

Potty-mouthed alternative club cum sweaty live music hole. Expect pan-stick-happy albinos in leather, students resplendent in retro, and owners of receding hairlines that should have burnt their Metallica T-shirts back when Kylie was still wearing dungarees. Musically you can expect goth, rock, techno and – dear God – nu-metal. Sexually you can expect frustration.

The Birdcage
52-56 Boar Lane (0113) 246 7273

A crazy club with crazy people, The Birdcage is home to the city's most sparkly drag artists and cheesiest playlist. The unabashed tongue-in-cheekiness means leaving your grumpy pants at the door and diving headfirst into unrestrained silliness. The punters are as chirpy and colourful as an aviary full of canaries, and can occasionally burst into spontaneous song in a music hall audience/ cock-er-ney sparrow stylee. Top tip for pulling? Take some millet with you.

Wed-Thu 9pm-2am, Fri-Sat 8pm-3am, Sun 9pm-1am
Wed 80p, Thu 90p before 9.30pm/£2 after, Fri-Sat free before 9pm/£3 before 10.30pm/£6 after

The Blank Canvas
Granary Wharf (0113) 244 6570

If you go down to the arches today you're in for a big surprise... Nestled beneath the train tracks lies one of the city's most eclectic live music and clubbing venues.. As the 10.23 to Blackpool North rumbles overhead, this 1,000 capacity venue plays host to superclub Federation and its team of outrageous entertainers, including members of the fashion police, go-go dancers, and drag queens who'll read you a bedtime story snuggled under a duvet. Its size also means it can sometimes pip the Cockpit to the post live music-wise, with acts like The Music, The Black Rebel Motorcycle Club and The Scissor Sisters setting up on its stage. Leave your pretensions at the door and prepare to go underground.

Federation: 1st Sat of the month, 10pm-4am; £12 advance (£10 members)/£15 door. See press for gig details

Bondi Beach Bar

City Square (0113) 243 4733

As the name indicates, this place is rather like the Baja Beach Club but with one notable difference. Both places have tanker-loads of cheap booze, lots of bikini girls and more numbskulls than you can wave a stick at – but only Bondi has the revolving dance floor. Quite why it has one is anyone's guess but a revolving door would be far more useful in this place... or even a loaded revolver.

Mon-Sat 5pm-2.30am, Sun 5pm-10.30pm
Mon-Wed free before 11pm/£2 after, Thu £5/£4, Fri-Sat £2 before 10pm/£3 before 11pm/£5 after

The Cockpit

Swinegate (0113) 244 1573

Buried deep beneath the railway station, The Cockpit is as dark and dingy as a rock club should be. It was Radio One's Best Live Music Venue of 2002 and since then has become one of the area's most popular gig venues. This subterranean music pit rocks like a rugby team bus with whores on the back seats when the right band is on stage, and top bands seem to be queuing up to play here. Club nights at The Cockpit are just as exciting and cater for all sorts of liberated, right-on dudes. There's a gay night, a punk night, an acoustic night and, er... a quiz night. Don't ask, just rock!

Bar: Mon-Sat 4.30pm-11pm
Tue 10.30pm-2.15am
Thu-Fri 11pm-2.30am, Sat 11pm-3am
Tue £3, Thu £2.50-£3.50, Fri-Sat £4-£5

Creation

52 Cookridge Street (0113) 224 0100

The debate's still out on whether size is important (Sex and the City says yes, Dear Deidre says no – at least not within a warm and loving relationship), but one thing's for sure – with Creation's square footage, escaping last week's unsavoury suitor has suddenly become a hell of a lot easier. In fact, with three different rooms/arenas, their differing music styles and a spookily segregated sound system, arguments of all kinds can be sorted out by walking a few dozen yards. Unfortunately, the advertised musical diversity of RnB, hip hop, house, chart, cheese and a "little bit of rock" is as homogenous as a carton of UHT. Which together with the hungry-handed male contingent made us more inclined to apocalypse rather than creation.

Wed 9.30pm-2am, Thu 9pm-3am,
Fri 9.30pm-2.30am, Sat 9pm-3am,
Sun 9pm-1am
Wed free b4 10pm/£4 after, Thu free b4 10pm/£2 b4 11pm/£3 after with flyer,
Fri £2 b4 10pm/£6 after (members £2 off),
Sat £2 b4 10pm/£8 after (members £6),
Sun £1 b4 10pm/£2 after

The Elbow Room

64 Call Lane (0113) 245 7011

Being the genial host that the Elbow Room is, not only can you shoot pool all day while indulging in some choice beers and gut-bustin' burgers, but come the evening they'll put on their favourite records and transform themselves into a funky nightspot and all for your absolute pleasure. The weekends are the real pull with Saturday's 'Sugarbeat

Club' earning itself a cast-iron reputation on the clubbing circuit, thanks to Utah Saints boys Jez and Tim drawing in the crowds with breaks, beats and electro bits and bobs. Always funky and unpretentious, you can even stick to the pool if rhythm's something that gave you a very wide berth when you popped into the world.

Mon-Thu 12pm-2am, Fri-Sat 12pm-3am,
Sun 12pm-12am
Sun-Fri free, Sat £5

Evolution

Cardigan Fields, Kirkstall
(0113) 263 2632

Out of town and off its head, you're unlikely to waste your taxi fare getting here if you're up for a raucous night of dancing and spending your chips on the fab selection of drinks offers. Saturday nights bring 'Jelly

Baby' with chart and party, RnB and funky house, while Thursday nights welcome the students in with open arms at the much revered 'Vodka', offering some cheesy tunes as well as the obligatory bucketfuls of spirits. They even do an under 18s night too, so you can get your younger sister on the party wagon before she starts hanging around with you. Attracting visiting TV stars, chart acts and Jo Guest, there's always a good night to be had, providing it's your thing – you know who you are.

Mon/Thu 10pm-2am, Sat 10pm-3am
Mon/Thu £3 b4 11pm, £4 after, Sat £5/£4
NUS & members
Visit website for other listings

The Faversham

Springfield Mount (0113) 243 1481
Like a cheeky tearaway who used to drag its mates away from school to drink cider in the park, The Fav has finally grown up, bought itself a decent record collection and developed a taste for lounging and drinking foreign beers. An impressive selection of nights make it worth the journey from day into evening, with Friday's funk, soul, breaks and beats-fest 'New Bohemia', and Saturday's 'Bad Sneakers' with live music and DJs, being two of the best. Never afraid to try something new, The Fav experiments with a mixture of live acts, DJs and genres, even handing the decks over to Leeds' producers and musicians in its monthly 'Re: Write' night. The Sunday sessions round off a great week of events with live acts soothing you through your Sunday roast.

Mon-Thu 12pm-2am, Fri-Sat 12pm-3am,
Sun 12pm-1am
Entry £3-£5 depending on the night

Federation

Blank Canvas, Granary Wharf
0870 122 0114

For something that only shows its face in the dark arches of Granary Wharf once a month, Federation is quite the brightest party ship on the horizon. Forget bopping half-heartedly to some lukewarm beats with an alcopop in your hand, here you'll find a fine array of DJs, dancers, stage shows, visuals and various entertainments and titillations along the monthly theme (anything from 'Jailhouse Cock' to 'Little Fed Riding Hood')

to keep the crowds coming back in their droves. A pre-party at Fibre and post-bash soiree at Mission round the night off nicely. Strictly for open-minded gay/straight folk who can't survive without a dose of camp and glam.

1st Sat of the month, 10pm-4am
£12 advance (£10 members)/£15 door

Flares

40 Boar Lane (0113) 205 1931

The 70s revival is an acquired taste, a bit like decking your homestead out like Blackpool illuminations over the festive period. Some people think it's all jolly good fun and others would rather spoon out their eyeballs than be assaulted by the garishness of it all. But at least Flares forewarns its punters, with a subtle 'Don't Walk – Boogie' sign blinking from its entrance. Once inside, the bevy of man-made fibres could run a small power station with the static they create, and on any one night there's at least 30 blokes bearing more than a passing resemblance to Dennis Waterman. If the disco soundtrack doesn't get your platforms moving, may we suggest a simple game of 'spot the trouser bulge'? Those skin tight Farahs were never the most flattering of styles...

Mon-Wed 8pm-12am, Thu 8pm-1am,
Fri-Sat 7pm-2am, Sun 7pm-12am
Mon-Thu & Sun Free, Fri-Sat £3 after
10.30pm

The Fruit Cupboard

50-52 Call Lane (0113) 243 8666

Stashed at the bottom of gold-paved Call Lane, the Fruit Cupboard is aptly named, partly because of its firm and fruity female clientele and partly because it's about the size of a cupboard. But don't let that put you off. Old Mother Hubbard was always first to the cupboard when it came to handing bones out, and who are we to say she was wrong? Try your luck on the cosy downstairs dancefloor where you can size up the knick-

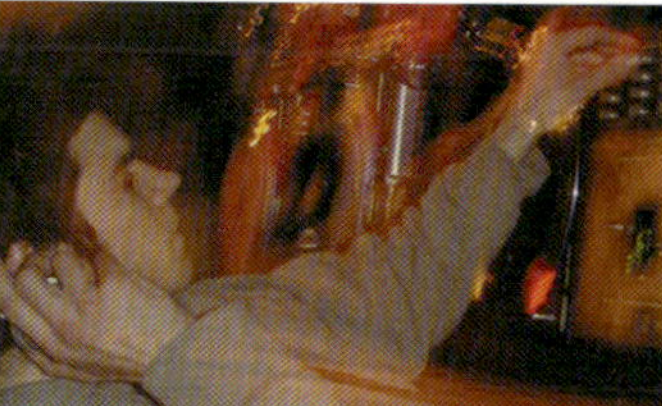

knack-paddy-whack talent before giving it all you've got with a big fat bone in your hand. Once she's seen your knick-knacks all you have to do is roll the old man home and everybody's happy... or something like that. Down Shep!

Mon 9.30pm-2.30am, Tue 10pm-2.30am,
Thu-Fri 10pm-late, Sat 10.30pm-4am
Mon 80p, Tue £2, Thu-Fri £4-£5, Sat £6-£8

MONDAYS
MONKEY BUSINESS
CHART & PARTY
DJ MARK SMITH
HIP-HOP & R'N'B
DJ ANTON
GREAT GAMES, MUSIC & ENTERTAINMENT
MONKEY BUSINESS
LEEDS BIGGEST STUDENT DRINKING CLUB
VODKA
NATIONWIDE
ITS BACK
TO ITS TRUE HOME!
EVERY THURSDAY
Evoluton Nightclub
Opposite VUE Cinema
Kirktall, Leeds.
Visit:
www.clubevolution.co.uk
E-mail:
team@clubevolution.co.uk
Call Us:
0113 263 2632
evolution
CLUB EVOLUTION PRESENTS...
floorfillers
every friday
the best dance & happy house
LEEDS' BIGGEST SATURDAY NIGHT PARTY
IN LEEDS' LARGEST NIGHTCLUB...
JELLY BABY SATURDAYS
SATURDAYS
COMMERCIAL DANCE & STUDENT ANTHEMS!
LEE CAMPBELL
RNB/HIP HOP
B NAUGHTY
FROM RADIO ONE'S 1Xtra
JELLY BABY
ABSOLUTE LEEDS
CLUBNIGHT OF THE MONTH
CLUBEVOLUTION.CO.UK

Heaven and Hell

Grand Arcade (0113) 243 9963

'Heaven and Smell,' as Leeds' least gifted satirists would have it, appears to be a bit of a misnomer these days as Heaven seems to have cashed in its shares and left old Hell with the run of the show. Divided into three levels – Hell, Purgatory and Heaven – there's little to distinguish each from the other, apart from altitude levels. They all stink. Even Beelzebub would give this one a swerve.

*Mon-Wed 9pm-2am, Thu 9pm-3am,
Fri-Sat 10pm-4am*
*Mon-Wed £3-£6, Thu 80p before 11pm, £3
after, Fri £10, Sat £12/£10*

HiFi Club

2 Central Road (0113) 242 7353

If a Bohemian artistic movement was to form in Leeds and sweep the nation in a cultural coup, it would begin in the HiFi Club. An impressive melange of jazz, hip hop, soul, funk, new wave, electro and motown nights, there's pretty much anything to choose from, just nothing that involves chucking glo-sticks around, and it'll always be the better for it. Minimalist, intimate and enduringly unique, guest DJs from far-flung lands and live acts often combine with the clubnights to give it an individual edge, and what HiFi doesn't play or put on its stage, probably isn't worth knowing about. Nights to watch out for are Pigs (monthly Tue), Move On Up (Wed) and FunkSoulNation (Fri) – but get there quick – HiFi's appeal is no secret.

*Mon/Wed 10pm-2am, Tue (times depends
on night), Thu 10pm-2.30am, Fri 10pm-
3am (also 6pm-10pm once a month), Sat
10pm-3am (comedy 7pm-10pm), Sun
12pm-12.30am*
*Mon/Wed £4/£3.50, Tue £3.50-£5 (depend-
ing on night), Thu £5/£4, Fri £6/£5,
Sat £6/£5 (comedy night £10 + entry to
clubnight), Sun free*

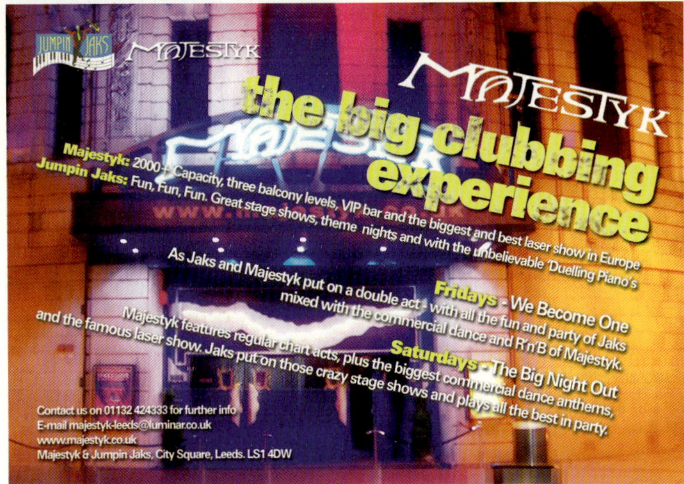

Jumpin' Jaks

Quebec Street (0113) 242 4333

As much as we'd hate to sound like our mother, wouldn't it be boring if we all liked the same thing? The indie kids can fill their baggy pants with Britpop classics at The Cockpit, the ravers and house brigade will be happy enough at Federation or Mission and those up for something funkier can set up camp in the HiFi. For those who fancy something a bit cheesier, with drinks offers designed to get you clamouring to grab the mic and belt out a Barbra Streisand number, here's the spot. Linked to weekend Mecca Majestyk, there's a load of fun to be had in either, but Jaks is the spot if dancing to tunes you can sing to beats posing by the bar and waiting in vain for some hot young thing to slip you their number.

Thu 9pm-2am, Fri-Sat 8.30pm-2.30am, occasional Sun

Thu £2, Fri free b4 10pm/£2 with flyer/£4 without

Sat free b4 10pm/varies after (doors open between Jaks and Majestyks 12am)

No sportswear, you may be required to show valid ID

Kiss Da Funk @ Mission

It's about time Back2Basics had some decent competition, and Kiss Da Funk, beginning its 2nd year as 2005 kicks off, is certainly the one to make it wake up and smell the absinthe. Appearing at party centralis Mission on the last Friday of every month, it gets the arches pumping with house beats courtesy of resident duo the Trophy Twins and various guests. Nominated for the UK's best house night and best northern night in Mixmag, they scooped the award for the UK's sexiest crowd and decided to share the wealth with the rest of the country with parties in London, Passion in Coalville, Norwich and Garlands in Ibiza.

Last Fri of month, 10pm-5am £12/£8 NUS

Majestyk

City Square (0113) 242 4333

It may get more stick than a Sellotape factory, but come the weekend, Majestyk shows it's earned its place in the nightclub premiership and with a capacity and light show to rival Ibiza's most established night spots, it may even qualifies for the Champions League. On the downside, its size means you might lose your mates within five minutes and a trip to the bar, but after a few drinks, that might not be a bad thing. Not for the yuppies, and not for the faint hearted either, but for a boozy, reckless night out, there's no bigger or better than this.

Tue, Thu & Fri 10pm-2am, Sat 10pm-5am
Tue before 11pm £2.50/£3.50 after, Thu £3, Fri £14 (drinks free all night – £3 off for women, £1 off for men with flyer before midnight), Sat £6

Mission

Trevelyan Square 0870 122 0114

Set in a series of railway arches, but there won't be any tramps drinking White Lightening in this neck of the woods – no siree. Having swiftly established itself as the clubbing centralis du jour, Mission continues to be the darling of the moment by making sure it provides a great atmosphere, top DJs and a cracking range of nights. Check out Saturday fixture 'Housework' keeping the masses dancing through the night with no signs of let up to the likes of Judge Jules, Lisa Lashes and other commendable peddlers of hard dance, funk and disco. With separate arches commandeering different beats, you're guaranteed a top night out, whichever party you end up in.

Usually 10pm-4am, vary during the week
General admission is £10 with discounts for NUS and members

Mint Club

8 Harrison Street (0113) 244 3168

Get fresh for the weekend at the Mint with an impressive list of nights including Saturday's alternating duo 'Technique' and 'Asylum', or fill up with some chunky beats on a Friday courtesy of 'Mix-In', 'Quality Connects' or 'Naked Bassline'. Also home to the much revered 'Funky Wormhole', with such a smashing range of DJs and music on offer, it's no surprise that the townsfolk just can't keep themselves and their party dollars away. Funky décor along a mint theme and an intimate atmosphere make for a wicked night whatever the occasion.

Thu 10pm-3am, Fri 10pm-late, Sat 10pm-6am, check www.themintclubleeds.co.uk for full details of weekday events
Thu £4, Fri £3-£8, Sat £8-£10

MPV

**5-8 Church Street, Kirkgate
(0113) 243 9486**

The most unique address in Leeds, probably in all of Yorkshire, bar even those crazy golf ball things near Harrogate that George Bush likes to mess around with. More of a club/bar hybrid, its four red pods nestling under therailway arches certainly get folk talk-

ing, but their appeal is obvious sinceeven with its duff location, it manages to attract hordes of adoring drinkers. Inside it has a minimal yet futuristic feel, with the two middle pods providing a more chilled out vibe to the cocktail-supping, DJ-led atmosphere of the two outside chambers. Unisex toilets, a massive disco ball, and the sheer cleverness of the front-opening pods make for a quirky and always brilliant nightspot.
Thu-Sat 10pm-2am
Free

Space

Hirsts Yard (0113) 246 1030

"Space...the final frontier. These are the voyages of the Starship Enterprise. On a five year mission to seek out new planets and new civilizations... to boldly go where no man has gone before." Well... not quite, but those who boldly go through the doors of Space will quickly discover that just about the only thing that there isn't inside this club is, err... any space to move in. Also, the club's fondness for dry ice and an apparent lack of air conditioning leaves you feeling like you're wearing a Klingon cloaking device. It's a popular feature in student life, but student life, as they say, is "Life Jim, but not as we know it".
Tue 10pm-2am, Wed 10pm-3am,
Thu 10pm-2.30am, Fri-Sat 10pm-4am
Drinks promotions available
Mon-Thu £3-£5, Fri £5-£7, Sat £7-£10,
Sun £5-£8

Rehab

Assembly Street (0113) 223 7647

Probably the most inappropriately named club anywhere on the planet, Rehab is all about throwing caution to the wind, rather than physically and spiritually cleansing yourself towards a better place in life. Expect

a crowd of frosty fashion fillies who, over the course of the evening, magically metamorphose into incredibly friendly creatures with pupils the size of marbles. Saturday's signature night 'Back2Basics' cements the club's cool, bringing in the big names to play alongside residents Ralph Lawson, Dave

itchycities...
Glasgow
Edinburgh
Leeds
York
Manchester
Liverpool
Sheffield
Nottingham
Birmingham
Cambridge
Cardiff
Oxford
Bristol
London
Bath
Brighton
and now introducing...
itchy Cornwall
CORN WALL
www.itchycity.co.uk

Beer, Tristan Da Cunha, Paul Woodford, and James Holdroyd. We wouldn't make make any appointments for Sunday lunch.
Mon/Wed/Thu 10pm-2.30am,
Fri 10pm-4am, Sat 10pm-4am/6am,
monthly Sun 10pm-4am
Mon-Thu £3-£5, Fri £8-£10, Sat £10 before
11pm/£12 after, Sunday varies

The Wardrobe
6 St Peter's Buildings, St Peter's Square (0113) 383 8800

Once you've spent the evening being wined and dined at The Wardrobe's bar and restaurant, before heading downstairs to its funky club, never again will you queue in the brisk northern weather to get into a nightspot again. The perfect place for a spot of groovin', there's a cracking selection of live acts, DJs and unique club nights on offer. With its own bar to keep the fun well lubricated, this intimate nightspot will get your feet tapping to a range of funk, soul and hip hop acts, and being the principal host for Leeds Jazz in the city, you can be sure there'll be plenty of jazz on the event list too.

Club opening times vary, check website for details
Entry prices vary

Warehouse
19-21 Somers Street (0113) 246 8287

In today's cut and thrust world of nightclub management, it's rare to see a decent club last longer than ten years (and we're not counting your local Roxy's – which is only busy by default) before being usurped by a younger, sprightlier version of itself. So, let's wrap a satin cape around this long-time contender of the Leeds' scene and give it some raucous applause. From 1983's Frankie Goes To Hollywood gig to the current line-up of hard house, RnB, funk and disco, the Warehouse is still going strong. The legendary Speed Queen has returned home after its brief absence, and still remains the most fun you can have with your trousers on. Bring your glitter.
Fri 9pm-3am, Sat 10pm-4am
£8-£15

cafés

Brodicks

Corn Exchange (0113) 245 5190

After a hard morning of browsing baggy jeans and flicking through cult comics, take refuge on the Corn Exchange's subterranean level. Serving up a range of snacks, sandwiches, coffees and cakes, it's the perfect spot to lounge on the squidgy sofas and look up the skirts of the shoppers on the stairs. As if you'd do such a thing...

Mon-Sun 9.30am-5pm
Welsh mussels £5.95

Citrus Café

Corn Exchange (0113) 244 4809

As well as housing over 60 speciality retailers, the Corn Exchange is a prime spot for people watching. Learn more about the kids of today in five minutes than Grange Hill could teach you in a whole season. Sit back with a freshly squeezed juice to eye-up the city's young and beautiful working the latest trends.

Mon-Sun 9am-5pm
Chicken burger £4.75

Clock Café

16a Headingley Lane, Headingley (0113) 294 5464

Lucky recipient of a brand spanking new refurb, this Headingely stalwart is now so much more than a handy hangover spot. Decked out like Barbarella's front room, the sixties style seeps onto the pavement, where you can enjoy anything from breakfast to beef enchiladas to the roaring sound of Otley Road traffic. Groovy baby.

Mon-Sat 10am-12am (stop serving alcohol at 11pm), Sun 10am-10pm
Mini mezze platter £4.50

Crusty Bin

**5 The Parade, North Lane, Headingley
(0113) 275 2558**
Ok, a couple of plastic chairs don't constitute a café, but if you need something greasy and fried at an ungodly hour in the morning this is the place to go. Just don't blame us when your arteries harden.
Mon-Sun 5am-3pm
English breakfast £3

Dare Café

49 Otley Road (0113) 230 2828
Flanked by Headingley's army of estate agents, Dare is a welcome break from arguing with your future housemates over central heating and box-rooms. The reasonable prices mean the student fraternity can swap their usual beans for burritos, while the frosted front windows are handy for hiding from anyone you owe money to.
*Mon-Sun 9am-4.30pm (day menu)/
5.30pm-10pm (evening menu)*
Main meal and drink £6.45

Fat Chops Café Bar

396 Kirkstall Road (0113) 275 2266
Miles out of the city centre in the cultural wasteland of Kirkstall, this bright café is a handy stop-off after a morning perusing the spy shop. We recommend the hot chocolate – a brown velvety monster in a mug.
*Mon 10am-5pm, Tue-Fri 9am-5.30pm,
Sat 9am-5pm, Sun 11am-4pm*
Sandwiches £2.95

Harvey Nichols Espresso Bar

Victoria Quarter (0113) 204 8000
Although the Fourth Floor is billed as a bar, restaurant, and café, the thought of ingesting anything near all those designer labels made us come out in hives. A much more palatable option is the ground floor espresso bar, which lets you stare at the glamorous Victorian Arcade shoppers while you stuff your gob with a week's supply of calories.
*Mon-Wed 10am-6pm, Thu-Fri 10am-7pm,
Sat 9am-7pm, Sun 11am-5pm*
Whitby crab £9.50

Kadas

Crown Street (0113) 243 3433
Yorkshire's weather is about as far away from the humid climes of North Africa as is possible. But this sunny café will have you lounging on a rug and puffing on a shishah pipe before you can say 'Lawrence of Arabia'. Food comes hot and spicy, with plenty or veggie options and platters to share.
Mon-Sat 11am-late, Sun 12pm-1am
Toasted sandwich £3.50

gay

The Base
24-32 Bridge End (0113) 368 4648
Friendly pub/bar that attracts a good crowd of mixed ages and sexes, and one of the gems on the scene. Featuring a raised dancefloor that also doubles up as a stage for nights like Quiz Night (Wednesdays) and

Cabaret Night (Sundays), which is undoubtedly this venue's weekly highlight. Also deserves a special mention for the adventurous, gloriously camp décor, including the 'Melanie B Art Gallery'.
Sun-Thu 12.30pm-12am, Fri-Sat 4pm-2am
Food: Mon-Fri 12pm-2pm
Grilled tuna steak salad £4.95,
House wine £8.45

Blayde's
**Blayde's Yard, Lower Briggate
(0113) 244 5590**
Walk into this bar in the middle of a daydream and you'll think you've stepped back in time to a small country pub in the middle of the countryside, except in an alternative, extremely camp, universe. The tiny venue gets pretty cramped at night with crowds, though for what reason we really can't fath-

om. Also appears to be the place where old lesbians go to die, unfortunately.

Mon-Thu 2pm-11pm, Fri-Sat 2pm-1am,
Sun 2pm-12.30am
No food, House wine £2.60 (small bottles)

The Bridge
Bridge End (0113) 244 4734

Originally decorated as a 'proper pub' for locals, The Bridge has had a refurbishment in an effort to bring in a younger crowd (and more importantly their paper money-stuffed wallets). This hasn't really worked – someone should inform Mr Bridge that a lick of magnolia paint does not a style-bar make, and the old crowd have stayed regardless of the new 'décor'. Karaoke on a Thursday is always fun though.

Mon-Wed 12pm-12am, Thu 12pm-1am,
Fri-Sat 12pm-2am, Sun 1pm-12am
No food, House wine £3.10 (small bottles)

Fibre
168 Lower Briggate (0113) 234 1304

The trendy alternative to QC next door, Fibre attracts a mixed crowd of gay and straight, (the latter largely being of the female variety), united in their love of house music.

Full of beautiful, fabulous people, and cleverly glass-fronted to show the rabble on the outside exactly what they're missing. Also a very pleasant prospect during the day, when chilled-out tracks and a modern menu make for a very fab spot for hanging around in trying to chase off the hangover from the previous night's revelries.

Mon-Wed 11am-12am, Thu 11am-1am,
Fri-Sat 11am-2am, Sun 12pm-12am
Food: Mon-Sun 12pm-7pm
Oriental duck wrap £4, House wine £9.50

The New Penny
57 Call Lane (0113) 243 8055

Never before has a name been so inappropriate. The only new thing about this place was the look twisted onto my face when I tried to work out what kind of hellish place I'd walked into. What appears to be the male counterpart to Blayde's, is a local pub for local people through and through. Some folk will happily enjoy its aged feel, just not the hip young things that make up much of Leeds gay scene – sorry.

Mon-Tue 12pm-11pm,
Wed-Sat 12pm-2am, Sun 2pm-12.30am
No food, House wine £12

Queen's Court (QC)

Queen's Court, Off Lower Briggate
(0113) 245 9449

The aptly-monikered Queen's Court isn't so named because of the clientele, but actually after the 'historical' cobbled courtyard between the bar and neighbouring Fibre.

During the summer days, the courtyard really comes into its own as a handy place to munch some curly fires and sip a double vodka and Fanta Lemon (don't knock it 'til you've tried it). However, the fact that it's a bar trying to be a club is quite a sore point, and the far-from-ideal corridor shape of the venue means that it becomes frustratingly hard to navigate when busy. In fact, the song you got up to have a boogie to will probably have finished by the time you get to the (very sweaty) dancefloor. £1 per drink on Mondays is a big draw, along with the aforementioned curly fries. Unless Whitney Houston dance remixes are your bag.

Mon-Sat 12pm-2am, Sun 12pm-11pm
Food: Mon-Sat 10am-7pm, Sun 12pm-7pm
Rib-eye steak £5.95, House wine £6.40

Federation

Blank Canvas, Granary Wharf
0870 122 0114

Not technically a gay night, but a gay-friendly one that attracts about a 50% gay crowd of muscle Marys shaking their booties to house music in all its guises. Happening in the dark arches of the Blank Canvas once a month, but frankly, thank Christ for that – with a £15 door fee and a party as good as this one, we might forget to buy ourselves food every week if they ran the bash every seven days. Run by the team behind Fibre, expect an unsurprisingly gorgeous crowd, a glamorous vibe and cunning theme every month.

1st Sat of the month, 10pm-4am
£12 advance (£10 members), £15 door

Homo @ Mission, Heaton's Court

Strictly gay night at superclub Mission presented by former Mr Gay UK Harry French and Gaydar. Choose from commercial dance in arena 1 or cheesy pop from Poptarts in arena 2, hosted by Karl Lucas (ex Poptastic/ Homiesexual – Manchester), and enjoy the talents of DJs from some of the UK's leading gay clubs in arena 3. Always a wicked night, catch the pre-parties in The Base every week if you think you're man enough.

Thu 10pm-3am
£3

SpeedQueen @ The Warehouse

Legendary gay night that attracts anyone with an open mind, SpeedQueen's had a few home changes of late. But now it's happily

settled in at its old home The Warehouse, where it holds the party to end all parties every Saturday. Drag queens, live percussion, house on the decks and outfits that'll knock your socks off – be early and make an extra-special effort, or prepare yourself for queues longer than a drag queen's inside leg measurement.

Sat 10pm-4am

£8 members, £10 guests

Shops

Clone Zone

164 Briggate (0113) 242 6967

Your one-stop shop for all things gay, this place has been described as, among many things, a porn shop, a clothes shop, and a 'gay lifestyle' store. The truth is closer to the latter, but is more like a combination of the three, and all this in stylish and friendly surroundings.

Mon-Sat 11am-7pm, Sun 12pm-7pm

Resources

FFLAG (Friends & Families of Lesbians & Gays)

(01454) 852 418

www.fflag.org.uk

Leeds Uni LGBT Society

www.leedslgbt.co.uk
leeds_lgb@hotmail.com

Leeds Met LGB

www.geocities.com/leedsmetlgb
leedslgb@hotmail.com

Stonewall

(020) 7881 9440

Campaign group who lead crusades on most gay-related UK politics
www.stonewall.org.uk

Yorkshire MesMac

(0113) 244 4209

Local sexual health authority for gay men
www.mesmac.co.uk

shopping

• Highlights...

• Wandering round independent stalls on a Saturday in The Corn Exchange
• Finding enough to keep you occupied for a month in The Light
• Thu-Sat late opening hours in 'Leeds Alive After Five'

• Lowlights...

• St John's and The Merrion Centre '80s time warp centralis
• Not being able to afford clothes (or even biscuits) in Harvey Nic's
• The arcade that smells of wee next to House Of Fraser – euw

The Centre's
(The St John's, Merrion, and Headrow Centres)

If you're eager to start up your own Blazin' Squad or Girls Aloud, don't bother with a nationwide 'talent' search – just sign up the kids with the least acne that hang round here at the weekend. Armies of youths debate who's going to shoplift next from the bevy of high street staples on offer. Enter with caution, and try to keep your bearings – the automatic doors are your only chance of escaping outside.
Call for opening hours

The Light
The Headrow (0113) 218 2060
www.thelightleeds.co.uk

Like a Generation Game conveyor belt, The Light gives you everything you could ever need and plenty to keep you coming back (apart from maybe a sandwich toaster). Bringing together the cream of fashion, retail and leisure, it's home to the likes of O' Neill, Tiger of Sweden, Rockport, Bennetton, Mikey, The Body Shop and Confetti; as well as a whopping 13 screen cinema and Esporta Health and Fitness Club. Continue the fun into the evening with a great array of bars and restaurants, including nightclub/bar/restaurant Life, Maxi's Express and M.A. Potters. All situated centrally and on top of its very own secure car park, as much as we try, we just can't see how they fit it all in, but by 'eck they do.
Mon-Thu 6am-12.30am, Fri 6am-2.30am, Sat 8am-2.30am, Sun 8am-12.30am
Check stores for individual opening times

welcome to
the pleasure
zone
the ultimate for fashion...
for cuisine... for movies... for lifestyle...
The Headrow, Leeds, LS1   www.thelightleeds.co.uk
thelight
Leeds

The White Rose Centre

Dewsbury Road, Junc 28 M62
(0113) 229 1234

All the high street shops squeeze their heads under one umbrella here. You're sheltered from the rain and the spit of disenfranchised youths gobbing over balconies (it's a bit far out for non-drivers), but not from the city crowds. If the Littlewoods superstore fails to grab your attention, there's a handy full-size Sainsbury's and an HMV with even better offers than usual. Whoever sang 'I Wish It Could Be Christmas Everyday' has obviously never experienced the Dawn of The Dead -style body rush to get through the doors come December.

Mon-Wed 10am-8pm, Thu 10am-9pm,
Fri 10am-8pm, Sat 9am-7pm, Sun 11am-5pm

Shopping Areas

Briggate & The Arcades

Beautifully restored arcades containing independent boutiques and the top end of the high street stores. The Victoria Arcade is as far removed from crimpeline petticoats and coal mining as you can get – offering the latest designer names to those with designer lifestyles.

Call for individual opening times

The Corn Exchange

Call Lane (0113) 234 0363
www.cornx.net

Those with an eye for the individual thank their lucky stars every day for this magnificent domed building filled with over 35 independent shops, selling everything from jewellery and jeans to comics and condoms, with some fab gift and record shops thrown in for good measure. Weekends see the concourse fill up with independently-owned

stalls and designers working and selling their pieces. Great for buying your mum that bonsai tree she's always wanted, or a handmade picture of Clint Eastwood on canvas for your brother; never before has buying a unique gift for someone (or yourself – push the boat out) been such an easy task. A smashing spot for taking in some Victorian architecture, grabbing a bite in the downstairs café or having a leisurely mooch around, and most importantly avoiding the unimaginative chain drudgery that the city centre seems to attract.

Mon-Fri 10am-5.30pm, Sat 9.30am-6pm,
Sun 11am-4pm

CORN|XCHANGE

A SHOPPING + LIFESTYLE DESTINATION

40 FASHION, MUSIC + LIFESTYLE OUTLETS. 3 CAFE-BARS.

CALL LANE, LEEDS LS1   www.cornx.net

Granary Wharf

Canal Basin (0113) 244 6570

Underground lair of shops, cafés and restaurants. Visit at the weekend for craft stalls, entertainers and the many hide-and-seek options available under the arches.
Call for individual opeing times

Leeds Kirkgate Market

Vicar Lane (0113) 214 5162

Put that pasty down. Now. You're not getting any younger so it's time to start looking after yourself. Stock up on cheap fruit and veg here as well as bargain oven cleaner, daffodils, disco balls and general tat. Service comes with a smile and a 'taa luv' but the flat cap, blue rinse and bag on wheels are optional.
Mon-Fri 9am-5pm (Wed till 2pm)

Department Stores

Alders

22-26 Headrow (0113) 200 2500

The St Winnefred's school choir may have sung the praises of grandma, but I doubt they were as keen on her wardobe as they were of her propensity to hand out choco-late. Lovers of chunky knits and flattering blouses can browse the rails, but unless there's a 'youth brand' sale on or you need the loo, you could quite happily live without a visit here.
Mon/Wed 9am-5.30pm,
Tue 9.30am-5.30pm, Thu 9am-7pm,
Fri-Sat 9am-6pm, Sun 11am-5pm

Harvey Nichols

107 Briggate (0113) 204 888

Amazingly, the thrill of some guy in a top hat opening a door for you can still send shoppers into a heady daze. Leeds is very proud of this high fashion store, and the beautiful bits come courtesy of Marc Jacobs, Roberto Cavalli, Stella McCartney and Balenciaga, amongst others. In addition there's a fancy food market, beauty salon, restaurant and an army of staff ready to look down their heavily lacquered eyelashes at you if you even think of questioning the price tags.
Mon-Wed 10am-6pm, Thu-Fri 10am-7pm,
Sat 9am-7pm, Sun 11am-5pm

House Of Fraser

140-142 Briggate (0113) 243 5235

Debenhams got Sadie Frost's knickers, BHS got Atomic Kitten's halter necks, but when the queen of bling wanted a home for her sweat pants, House of Fraser got the gig. Apart from J-Lo's lurid range of hood wear, there's actually a great range of cosmetics, perfumes and some decent high street brands in here.
Mon-Wed/Fri 9am-5.30pm, Thu
9am-7pm, Sat-9am-6pm, Sun 11am-5pm

www.itchycity.co.uk

TKMaxx

27 Albion Arcade (0113) 246 7990

One day people will realise that Britain's grey skies are not conducive to neon bright leisurewear. TKMaxx is home to the casual wear the designers would rather forget. Dig deep at this jumble sale of designer names and you may find some FCUK sandals, Gucci sunglasses or Polo sweatshirts. If not, there are plenty of outfits perfect for a Footballer's Wives fancy dress party.

Mon-Sat 9am-5.30pm, Sun 11am-5pm

Unisex

Ace

9 Duncan Street (0113) 245 4555

The window bursts with those hideous homewares that are now ironically hip. Unfortunately, without the expensive loft apartment to go with them, those beaded curtains will just be seen as bad taste. Instead, fill your wardrobe with cool clobber and button badges and just never invite anyone round.

Mon-Thu 10.30am-5.30 pm,
Fri-Sat 10am-6pm

Accent

Men's 11-13 Queens Arcade
(0113) 243 1707
Women's 18-20 Queens Arcade
(0113) 243 2414

Ouch. Did you feel that? Style just jumped up and smacked you in the face. Don't just stand there and take it – take charge. Snap up those feisty fashions and show them who's boss by parading their pretty faces (and yours) all around town.

Mon-Sat 9.30am-5.30pm, Sun 11am-4pm

Ark

Corn Exchange (0113) 244 4900

The latest in street wear from the likes of Bench, Hooch, Carhartt, Paul Frank and Miss Sixty. Unlike in the animal kingdom, the girl's stuff is far more colourful than the boy's.

Mon-Sat 9am-5.30pm, Fri-Sat 10am-6pm

Diesel

57-59 Vicar Lane (0113) 242 1719

The uniform for today's trendy types – but price-wise a real hike up from the M&S checked number I wore at school. Renowned for its jeans of many washes, cuts and colours and that ripped-to-perfection look.

Mon-Sat 9am-6pm, Sun 11am- 4.30pm

Exit

Corn Exchange (0113) 246 9301

When monkeys rule the world they'll plant bananas on every street corner, make us drink tea for their amusement, and buy all their clothes from Paul Frank. In fact, the monkey-loving designer may be the only one of us to survive. Get ready to pledge your allegiance to the primates now and stock up on his accessories and novelty wear here. If you don't believe us, you get trainers and skate wear without animals on too.

Mon-Sat 9.30am-5.30pm, Sun 11am-4.30pm

Faces and Names

59 Otley Road, Headingley
(0113) 230 4100

If you can justify a new outfit, but can't justify the bus fare into town, this shop brings stylish designer wear to the doorstep of Leeds students. There's even a bench across the way so poorer students can sit and stare gooey-eyed at the windows without being asked to move on.

Mon-Sat 10am-6.30pm, Sun 10am-4pm

Flannels

68 Vicar Lane (0113) 234 9977

We may pretend to be all right-on and 'of the people' but deep down we'd love to have an army of assistants pandering to our every whim and people in the street showing us the respect we really deserve. The assistants here won't help you fulfill those fantasies but they will sell you suitable designer clobber for bossing people about in.

Mon-Fri 9.30am-5.30pm, Sat 9am-6pm, Sun 11am- 4.45pm

H&M

129 Briggate (0113) 236 4740
Leeds Shopping Plaza, Albion Street
(0113) 380 0800

It could stand for 'Hit & Miss', but with their bargain prices and so many pieces to browse through, it's impossible to make a bad buy here. Get up-to-date fashion, accessories and undies and if you don't feel the same about that peach puff ball skirt once home, you'll only be a fiver down and it can always double as a tea towel.

Mon-Thu 9am-5.30pm, Fri-Sat 9am-6pm, Sun 11am-5pm

Hip

9/14-16 Thornton's Arcade
Men's (0113) 242 4617
Women's (0113) 234 7655

With custom trainers, Duffer, Adidas, Evisu, and Stussy to name but a few. this shop is cool in its purest form.

Mon-Sat 10am-5.30pm

O'Neill
The Light, The Headrow (0113) 245 5114

Everything you need for action-packed trips with those big tall skateboard things with no wheels. Even if the thought of sand/snow between your toes makes you long for the indoors, they also stock plenty of everyday wear alongside the practical stuff for the professionals.

Mon-Wed/Fri 9am-6pm,
Thu/Sat 9am-7pm, Sun 11am-5pm

Vivienne Westwood
15 County Arcade (0113) 245 6403

Her shoes may look like the modern equivalent of foot binding to some but her eccentric English fashions have graced the catwalk since the heady days of punk. Beautiful non-conformist pieces that look divine on curvy girls and sexy on skinny boys.

Mon-Sat 10am-6pm

Zoot
29 Otley Road, Headingley
(0113) 278 1692

Student wear at student prices, including Playboy, Peter Werth, Killah and Hooch.

Mon-Fri 9.30am-6pm, Sun 11am-5pm

Aqua
Corn Exchange (0113) 243 3336

Like cooking and child rearing, when you put a little love into making clothes it shows. Skinny, trendy types should prepare to fight for the outfit they've always dreamed of here. No hair pulling – the bald look is so not now.

Mon-Sat 10am-5.30pm, Sun 12pm-4pm

Can Can Boutique
Corn Exchange (0113) 245 2552

I can look great, I can, I can! Handbags down girls there's enough for all of you. Stylish, cool clothing for those tired of the high street shops.

Mon-Sat 10.30am-5.30pm, closed Sun

Dawn Stretton
30 Central Road (0113) 244 9083

While you and I created a humble tea towel in home economics, Dawn Stretton probably rustled up a set of oven gloves and apron to match. An expert with the old needle and thread, she's been whipping up red carpet creations for the likes of Louise Redknapp and Melinda Messenger for years now. Lots of sweeping skirts, fitted bustiers and shiny fabrics for those special occasions.

Mon-Sat 9.30am-5.30pm, Sun 11am-5pm

Ginger Ink (Women)

19b North Lane, Headingley
(0113) 278 9944

Headingley's charity shops may be your usual haunts, but step inside this boutique and discover what the stylish are wearing today, not thirty years and five hip operations later. Unfortunately, the prices aren't as flattering as the clothes. Damn.

Mon-Sat 10am-6pm

Oasis

Commercial Street (0113) 243 2336

Pass that girl outside the window a tissue – she's drooling. Feminine fashion and affordable accessories that'll have you hitting people with your handbag to get to. Accidentally of course.

Mon-Fri 9.30am-5.30pm, Sat 9.30pm-6pm, Sun 11am-5pm

Tunnel

22 Queens Arcade (0113) 243 9996

My midget grandma is always saying that good things come in small packages, but as we all know, in real life it's the big fuck-off box under the Christmas tree that everyone's interested in. To reset the balance, this teeny tiny shop packs in the fashion goodness by the truckload. And you don't have to be vertically challenged to enjoy it.

Mon-Thu 9.30am-5pm, Fri-Sat 9.30am-5.30pm

Vicky Martin

42 Victoria Quarter (0113) 244 1477

The inevitable weight loss that comes with a bad break up should have you squeezing into one of these sexy little numbers and showing him what he's missing. Just remember to look suitably bored when he decides you really are the one for him, before leaving with that six-footer in the Armani suit.

Mon-Sat 10am-6pm

Men's

Aspecto

1 Queen Victoria Street (0113) 245 0150

It is possible to bridge the precarious gap between trainers and tie-ups. Aspecto's on hand to swathe your feet in style and comfort with brands like Camper, Carharrt and Etnies. Pop downstairs for clothes from Schott, Evisu and Duffer.

Mon-Sat 9am-6pm, Sun 11.30am-4.30pm

CITY CENTRE LEEDS
ALIVE AFTER 5

DON'T RUSH LUNCH WE'RE
OPEN
LATE

MORE SHOPS
MORE CHOICE
MORE TIME

SHOP 'TIL 7PM EVERY THURSDAY FRIDAY SATURDAY

Chimp

5 Thortons Arcade (0113) 234 9979

Effortlessly street style that's not actually effortless, and staff too cool for school. For funky designer clothes that you don't see all the regular hood rats and dizzy rascal wannabes in, you'd go ape if you knew what you were missing out on.

Mon-Sat 9.30am-5.30pm

Envy

97 Briggate (0113) 245 8045

Clothes that aren't about to spark jealous rages from your mates but will stop you from walking around with your nuts on show.

Mon-Tue 9am-5.30pm, Wed-Sat 9am-6pm, Sun 11am-5pm

Ginger Ink (Men)

26 Otley Road (0113) 278 9944

As tempting as it may be to spend your student loan buying every girl in The Oak a drink, when they're putting in the requisite five minutes saying thank you, you don't want them stifling laughter at your BHS T-shirt. Which is why the first thing you should do with the government's pay cheque is get yourself some new threads and let the ladies come to you. Saying that, the stuff here's not that expensive, so maybe you can buy the next round after all.

Mon-Sat 10am-6pm, Sun 12pm-5pm

Second-hand

Blue Rinse

11 Call Lane (0113) 245 1735

Some people still have hang ups about trying on someone else's jocks but I say you have to come off your overpriced high horse

and have a gander at some vintage style. Jackets, jeans, cords and T-shirts – all with an individualistic twist and at bargain prices. It's worth mentioning that a lot of ladies find the men in here attractive – this isn't an invite for singles though.

Mon-Fri 10.30am-6pm, Sat 10am-6pm, Sun 11am-4.30pm

The Final Curtain

Headingley Lane (no phone)

Vintage doesn't necessarily mean something in bri-nylon from the 70s. This tiny jumble sale of a shop has hidden within its depths designer pieces from the 1930s. So next time Stephen Fry is creating a movie about the roaring 20s, you can sashay in to the audition in a smoking jacket from that very era.

Tue-Sat 11am-5.30pm

Positively 13'O Clock

7a Crown street (0113) 243 2776

If you've had enough of just nodding along to the beats of Sly and the Family Stone, this place will have you looking the part and living the dream.

Mon-Thu 11am-5.30pm, Fri-Sat 11am-6pm

Rebop/Retro Clothing
Corn Exchange (no phone)

Want a T-shirt only you can sport? Want a slogan only you can express? Well, despite your dubious self-esteem issues, you'll find your refuge downstairs at the Corn Exchange. Used T-shirts start from a fiver and the retro shirts, flares and jackets should help top off your ensemble.

Mon-Sat 9.30pm, Sun 11am-4pm

Sugar Shack
14 Headingley Lane (0113) 226 1020

Not just for slow-witted folk who need to be reminded of their postcode via LS6-emblazoned clothing. This is the premier spot for students on a fancy dress mission. Although the giant afros certainly make a statement (and are a much wiser option than attempting the look with a home perm kit and a bottle of tequila), you're likely to spend the next few weeks picking up strange curly hairs from your carpet.

Mon-Sat 10am-6pm

Office
74 Briggate (0113) 247 1112

The coolest footwear on the block – from polka-dot peep toes to old skool sneakers – now all you have to do is find the outfit to match. Two words of warning though: wear good socks cause no-one needs to see those holey Mr Happy numbers, and don't try ordering anything – your shoes could leave and re-enter the fashion cycle by the time they arrive.

Mon-Wed/Fri-Sat 9am-6pm,
Thu 9am-7pm, Sun 11am-5pm

Size?
49/51 Vicar Lane (0113) 243 2221

Not the cheapest place to get your feet covered, but if you're a trainer fetishist looking for the perfect pair to bring your collection into the hundreds this is the place. Also stocks clothes and bags to complement your neat feet.

Mon-Wed 9.30am-6pm,
Thu-Sat 9.30am-6.30pm, Sun 11am-5pm

Blackwell's
21 Blenheim Terrace (0113) 243 2446

Solely responsible for saving the academic career of many an undergraduate, this Mother Theresa of the book world is your first stop for course texts the night before your exams. Handily located next door to a cashpoint, for when you really can't

resist their latest edition of 'Engineering Superconductivity'.
Mon-Sat 9am-5.30pm, Sun 11am-5pm

Borders

94-96 Briggate (0113) 242 4400

Forget travelling, the Internet or the national Census. The easy way to find out about your fellow man is a lengthy browse through Border's magazine section. From Skin Deep to SFX, the ideas and interests of every generation are covered here. If staring at complete strangers isn't your thing, they also stock books, DVDs and CDs aplenty.
Mon-Sat 9am-9pm, Sun 11am-5pm

Oxfam Books

**9 Otley Road, Headingley
(0113) 274 3818**

Students like good causes. They also read books. So where do Headingley-based students get rid of their key reading material once the learning's over? Here. Normal folk can browse an impressive selection of fiction and non, and although it's not as cheap as some charity shops, it's (altogether now) all for charity.
Mon-Sat 9.30am-5pm, Sun 11am-3pm

Waterstone's

36-38 Albion Street (0113) 242 0839
93 Albion Street (0113) 244 4588

If your local newsagent is Barry McGuigan, Waterstone's is Lennox Lewis. Not because they take part in organised violence, but because it's at the top of its field – a heavy weight of the book world. A stock list to keep you in holiday reads for a lifetime, a handy ordering service and friendly staff that'll call you when your book arrives. Don't try calling back for the softly spoken girl though – tried that, she's married.
Mon-Fri 8.45am-8pm, Sat 8.45am-6.30pm, Sun 11am-5pm

WHSmith

3-7 Lands Lane (0113) 242 2505
City Station (0113) 243 3059

The real traveller's friend. Grab a copy of Heat, the latest John Grisham and a packet of Liquorice Allsorts for that train journey ahead. The city centre branch has the nostalgic smell of stationery that'll take you back to those misspent school days.
Mon-Sat 8am-6pm, Sun 11am-5pm
Mon-Sat 6.30am-8.30pm, Sun 7.30am-8.30pm

Music

Choonz Worldwide

100-102 Vicar Lane (0113) 244 9966

To all those who make a T gesture with their hands when Faithless' Insomnia kicks in – this place is for you. Flick through the classic dance vinyl in store or use their nifty online mail order service.

Mon-Sat 10am-6pm

Crash

The Headrow (0113) 243 6743

For the bargain price of nought pence, you can promote your band's gig here – however small it may be (it's what you do with it that counts). And while you're watching your flyer being Blu-Tacked to the wall, pick up some inspiration from the racks of quality music.

Mon-Fri 9.30am-6pm, Sat 9am-6pm

HMV

1 Victoria Walk (0113) 245 5548

Vinyl, videos, CDs, DVDs, books, games, magazines and the annual Hollyoaks calendar. If you don't see the lifetime of entertainment options in this store, you possess a brain way beyond normal human capacity and need to spend your time inventing the fuzz-free peach or something.

Mon-Sat 9am-6pm, Sun 11am-5pm

Jumbo

Unit 5, St John's Centre, Merrion Street (0113) 245 5570

I'm nodding my head, I'm tapping my feet, I'm clicking now, I'm definitely feeling it, my legs are going crazy. Yes I'm in the groove but I'm still in the shop so I'm leaving with

my head down in shame. Buy your tickets, promote your band and get quality music at reasonable prices – just don't start dancing round the shop.

Mon-Fri 9.30am-5.30pm, Sat 9am-5.30pm

Music Zone

69 Briggate (0113) 245 4811

A great place to complete your music back catalogue on a budget. Cut-price chart CDs as well as the odd DVD and book. Some of the older releases are so cheap (a fiver a CD) you could start using them as coasters – at last, a practical use for Robbie William's work.

Mon-Fri 9am-5.30pm, Sat 9am-6pm,
Sun 11am-5pm

Out of Step

7 Crown Street (0113) 245 1730

Hip hop, rock and skater sounds to shake your head madly to – avoid if you suffer from persistent dandruff.

Mon-Sat 10am-6pm

Play Music

Corn Exchange (0113) 243 2777

Don't worry, they won't keep you in the shop till you bang out a few notes on a

bent penny whistle – the name's more of a suggestion really. Should you feel inspired though, they sell all the latest vinyl releases and imports for DJs who know their tunes and aren't afraid to use them.
Mon-Sat 10.30am-5.30pm

Polar Bear

4-5 Grand Arcade (0113) 243 8231
21a North Lane, Headingley (0113) 230 7232
There are times when your cup runneth over and times when your cup's so empty you've started using it for storing your loose change. When you're in the red, pick up some bargain second-hand CDs here. When you're in the black, sell them all back again and narrowly avoid reconstructive surgery courtesy of the debt collectors.
Mon-Sat 10am-5.30pm
Mon-Sat 10am-6pm, Sun 10am-5pm

Rock Shack

Cardigan Road (0113) 230 6363
Grab a guitar and set up your very own School of Rock.
Mon-Fri 10am-6pm, Sat 11am-6pm,
Sun 12pm-5pm

Virgin Megastore

Albion Street (0113) 243 8117
I don't think everyone realises, but if it weren't for places like Virgin, kids these days would be spending their cash on pellet guns and lighter fluid. Thanks to Virgin and its dizzying array of music, films and games, 13-year-old Perry can discover the delights of The Durrutti Column with his Christmas vouchers and 15-year-old Janice can experience the films of Pedro Almodavar with her pocket money. Give that shop a knighthood.
Mon 8am-6pm, Tue-Sat 9am-6pm (Thu till 7pm), Sun 11am-5pm

Other Cool Shops

Anti-Gravity

Upper Level, Corn Exchange
(0113) 244 3592
Sells everything for wind-assisted fun except whoopee cushions. Kit yourself out with kites, dune buggies, and juggling parephenalia.
Mon-Sat 10am-5.30pm, Sun 11am-4.30pm

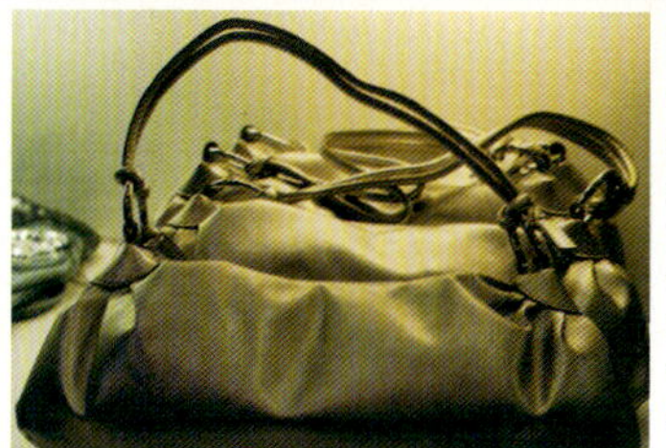

Atticus

**4 The Cresent, Hyde Park
(0113) 230 2989**

Earrings and handbags and sparklies for glad-rags,
Cards of all sizes and gifts for surprises.
Frames and neat notebooks, some bracelets, some rings,
These are a few of our favourite things...
Mon-Sat 10.30am-5pm/5.30pm

K.O.O.L.

Corn Exchange (0113) 246 9210

Opened in September 2004, here's the place to drop hints about when it approaches Valentine's day and you're expecting something special. Stocking a striking range of jewellery, handbags and clothes, the shop also holds exclusive rights for Yorkshire for many top designers in the field, including Trinny and Susannah favourite Butler and Wilson. Renowned for their high quality pieces that make the prices more than reasonable, and with Big Brother's Justine Sellman at the helm, you'll get a bit of star quality into the bargain too.
Mon-Sat 10am-5.30pm, Sun 12pm-4pm

Love it

Corn Exchange (0113) 247 1911

Cheap, funky accessories for the girl who goes out with that guy in the band. Pretty hairclips, chunky rings and plastic baubles to update your tired old T-shirt and jeans. See that girl who keeps pulling her hair back to show off her earrings? That could be you.
Mon-Sat 10am-5.30pm

Octopus

7 Queens Arcade (0113) 234 2605

Plain, inoffensive kitchenware is for boring, middle-aged sell-outs. Get a day-glo, cartoon-emblazoned toaster here and set up camp in middle youth forever.
Mon-Sat 9.30am-5.30pm, Sun 11am-4pm

Org Organics

79 Great George Street (0113) 234 7000

You might think that nervous twitch you've strangely acquired was the result of your headfirst dive off the steps of McDonalds, but it might well be because of all those nasty pesticides you keep eating with your

**CITY CENTRE LATE NIGHT SHOPPING
THURSDAY TO SATURDAY UNTIL 7PM**

★ WANTED ★

WORDSMITHS*

RECKON YOU WRITE RIVETING REVIEWS?

Go to www.itchycity.co.uk
or email iwritegood@itchymedia.co.uk

Each week, one review will win a boxset.
What's more, we'll put the best comments
in the itchy guides 2006

*NO COWBOY

iceberg lettuce. Org Organics will spank your ass with a 10 kilo organic marrow and get you eating good, clean, natural food in no time. Their shop will see you right if you're in town, but their home delivery service will get all that Gillian McKeith-endorsed stuff you saw on telly to your house, before you can say 'alfalfa sprout sandwich'.

Mon-Fri 9.30am-5.30pm, Sat 10am-5pm

Rose and Co

13 Thortons Arcade (0113) 254 701

Pretty pink potions and sparkling, lacy bits and pieces. How we imagine a Wild West whorehouse to look – in a heaving corset, marabou feather kind of way; not in a sleeping with men for money stylee.

Mon-Sat 9am-5.30pm, Sun 12pm-4pm

Scoot-A-Bout

Cardigan Road (0113) 278 7078

Listen dad, my feet are sore, and I can't afford to be living in taxis. You got me a bike for my 10th birthday and I'm not cheeky enough to ask you for a car or anything. It's just that a scooter would be a really sound investment and you know you'd want to have a go... Dad? Dad?... That's a no then is it?

Mon-Sat 9am-5pm

Space NK

63 Vicar Lane (0113) 242 6606

You could try liquidising a copy of Vogue, a £50 pound note and a bottle of pink Cristal in a blender, but if you're really after chic in a bottle come here. All the promising potions and pampering powders the stars plaster on their faces.

Mon-Wed 10am-6pm, Thu-Sat 9am-6pm, Sun 12pm-5pm

Travelling Man

Corn Exchange Balcony (0113) 242 7227

If you want to join an underground scene, forget clubbing in disused slaughterhouses or spraying graffiti on old trains – join the new comic revolution instead. One of our favourite shops in the city, Travelling Man stocks enough comics, graphic novels, collectables and games to fill a thousand rainy afternoons. We can't recommend 'The Adventures of Sock Monkey' enough.

Mon-Fri 9.30am-5.30pm, Sat 9am-5.30pm, Sun 11am-4.30pm

entertainment & culture

Live Music

Brudenell Social Club
33 Queens Road (0113) 275 2411
This kitsch little den is still hot from last year's not-so-secret Franz Ferdinand gig. A favourite of soon-to-be-signed indie darlings, think beer mats, dominos, and G & T's served in wine glasses.
Gigs from 7.30pm/8pm
From £5

The Cockpit
Swingate (0113) 244 1573
Voted 'Best Live Venue' by Radio 1 back in 2002 (something they've been milking ever since), this is still the best place in Leeds for live music. And after the strumming's over, the club nights deliver everything from hairy-toed mosh muzak to 80s classics, punk, and preening gay pup pop in a trucker cap.
Gigs from 7.30pm/8pm
From £4-£16

HiFi Club
2 Central Road (0113) 242 7353
A comedy session, various DJs, and a live music programme to rival most other gig spots in the city – it's a wonder those chaps

at the HiFi club have time to sleep. What used to be mainly centered on jazz and funk acts now encapsulates the indie/alternative scene with nights like 'PIGS' and 'Teatime Shuffle', and newcomer 'Off The Hook' representing urban talent. For the jazz fanciers old favourites 'The Harlem Bush Club' and 'Sunday Joint' bring in the cream of the UK's jazz, funk and soul acts, and there's always a healthy selection of visiting DJs for those who like their grooves without guitars.

Gigs from 10pm (Sun jazz from 1pm – free)
£4-£5

Joseph's Well

Chorley Lane (0113) 203 1861

Blending traditional pub décor with the edgy fashion stylings of its clientele, this live music stalwart is a sticky but charming place. It's more or less open plan, so it's easy to grope the big acts as they mix with the 'commoners', if you so wish. Local talent is always strumming away in here and the gigs are dirt-cheap.

Gigs from 7.30pm/8pm
From £3

Leeds Metropolitan University Students Union

Woodhouse Lane (0113) 283 2600

There are two schools of thought gig-wise. 1) Sanitised stadium rock with clear sight lines and adequate toilet facilities, and 2) loud, sweaty crushes in dark rooms where communication relies on sign language and anyone under five foot can only see the top of the lighting rig. This is the latter. Embrace for bands like Electric Six, Roots Manuva, Biffy Clyro, and The Beta Band.

Gigs from 7.30pm
From £6

Leeds University Refectory

Woodhouse Lane (visit CATS for tickets)

Along with the LMU, this is Leeds' biggest live music venue. Expect acts along the lines of The Thrills, The Hives, The NME Tour, and Athlete. Stop spending your cash on cheap pasta and stir-in sauces and stock up on band T-shirts and stickers instead.

Gigs from 7.30pm/8pm
Approx. £12.50-£20

The Pack Horse

208 Woodhouse Lane (0113) 245 3980

One of those pubs that looks like it's ready

for demolition but refuses to give it up and become one of those classy yellow places with scary ghost faces everywhere. Upstairs is the nicotine-drenched gig venue, complete with sweaty atmosphere and a splendidly mouthy crowd.

Gigs from 7pm/8pm
£2-£5

The New Roscoe

Bristol Street, Sheepscar
(0113) 246 0778

The one to watch for the best upcoming bands, some old bint in a blond wig stabbing Blondie's back catalogue to death with a kitten heel and the occasional big act. Otherwise it's business as usual with beer, boobs and the obligatory stuffed animals (?) adorning the walls and giving you 'the eye'. Call Jumbo Records on (0113) 245 5570 for tickets.

Gigs from 8pm
£4-£11

The Vine

The Headrow (0113) 203 1820

The Vine has had indie-lovin' fringe-wearers flicking imaginary fluff off their jumpers since it started hosting gigs last in 2003. Dirty boys with dirty hair and dirty Converse macarena to the best in indie, punk, rock, roll, and sleazy electro beats. Normal pub folk should be warned that when there's a gig on you'll have to pay entrance to the pub – but that's because it's kind of one big room, not because they're saving for a new fridge freezer.

Gigs Mon-Sat 6pm-11pm,
Sun 4pm-10.30pm
£3-£4

The Wardrobe

6 St Peter's Buildings, St Peter's Square
(0113) 383 8800
www.thewardrobe.co.uk

There's plenty in the city to keep the indie kids tapping their feet, but for the soul, funk and jazz fanatics, there's only The Wardrobe that's worth getting acquainted with. With live music filling up the café bar and downstairs club almost every night of the week, the cream of the local music scene is well-represented and there's plenty of UK and international acts keeping the music bill buzzing. Whether it's a laid-back cocktail session to a background of a touring jazz band or a full-on funk fest till the early hours – add this place to your aural favourites.

Check website for listings
Entry prices vary

Become a freelance A&R geezer and start schmoozing the 'next big things' at dingy student fave, The **Royal Park** (Royal Park Road – 0113 275 7494). The nearby **Fenton** (Woodhouse Lane – 0113 2453908) also has the odd aural experience, but you'll need ear plugs if you want to save your hearing from the atrocious PA system. For the cutting-edge of live music (i.e. three cords and a tambourine), check out the open mic specials at Dr Wu's (Call Lane 0113 242 7629) and for music that was popular 25 years ago, **The Primrose** (280 Meanwood Road – 0113 262 1368) plays punk for women with tie-dye skirts and red wine-stained gnashers. **The Grove** (Back Row, Holbeck – 0113 243 9254) is the place for eating unusual crisps and stroking your kneecaps to folk, and classical buffs can applaud ex-Moomin and joanna slapper Jamie Cullum at **Leeds College of Music** (3 Quarry Hill – 0113 222 3400). **Norman** (p 35) is the best place for catching live turntable wizadry, with DJs every night except Mondays.

Theatres

City Varieties

Swan Street (0113) 243 0808

Cor blimey gov'nor, apples and pears, Barbara Windsor's breasticles, jazz hands, chimney sweeps, yada, yada, yada. That's an old style music hall to you and me – expect kids and variety shows, as well as the odd comedy turn.

Evenings from 7.30pm
£6-£15

Civic Theatre

Cookridge Street (0113) 214 5315

Home to a striking Victorian décor and the occasional decent orchestra, but rarely pulls in the big guns.

Matinees from 2pm, Evenings from 7pm
From £6

Grand Theatre & Opera House

46 New Briggate (0113) 222 6222

If a big West End musical's in town, it'll be unpacking its tap shoes and backcombing its wigs in the dressing rooms here. Also home to an annual panto ("Oh no it isn't..." etc, etc).

Evenings from 7pm
£8.50-£50

Leeds Metropolitan University Theatre

Woodhouse Lane (0113) 283 5998

It's at this point we usually make a tired joke about affected drama students tearing at their hair and screaming in Polish, but aside from the odd over-experimental piece, this is where the stage stars of tomorrow cut their theatrical teeth.

Evenings from 7.30pm
Adults £7, Conc. £5

West Yorkshire Playhouse
Playhouse Square (0113) 213 7700

Regarded as one of the best regional theatres in the country, the WYP hosts the cream of new productions, both in-house and touring. Drama, dance, comedy and kids are all covered and their innovative marketing campaigns have seen new bums on seats year after year. The eclectic programme means even those scarred by sixth form Shakespeare will be tempted to give theatre one last chance.

Evenings from 7pm, matinees and signed performances also available
From £7 (standby tickets available)
£5 tickets: Mon-Wed for under 26s, midweek matinees for OAPs on Income Support

Independent Cinema

Leeds International Film Festival
Every Oct

Make sure you check out Leeds' very own version of Cannes (minus the camera-wielding pepperami and Dave Stewart pimping the Appleton sisters.) Discover Bollywood, indie and foreign cinema, then go straight back to the soul-sucking action flicks you usually watch.
www.leedsfilm.com

Cottage Road Cinema
7 Cottage Road (0113) 275 1606

Despite running reels since 1912, this independent cinema still hasn't succumbed to a playlist of boring blockbusters and cartoons about talking koalas. Although slightly more mainstream than the Picture House, they pick the most interesting new releases and have maintained that old-fashioned Saturday afternoon cinema vibe.
Mon-Sun 6pm, 8pm
Sat-Sun 11am (Sat only), 2pm & 4pm

Hyde Park Picture House
Corner Brudenell Road (0113) 275 2045

Fantastic alternative to the city's overpriced, spaceship-esque conveyer belt cinemas. This original Victorian building may be showing signs of wear and tear, but it's a portal to a world away from the Orlando Bloom happy/sad school of acting. Dip into an eccentric range of cult classics and independent films.

Mon-Thu 6pm/9pm,
Fri 6pm/8pm/10pm,
Sat 12pm/4pm/6pm/8pm/10pm,
Sun 4pm/6pm/8pm
Adult £4 (stalls)/£4.50 (balcony),
NUS £3.50, Friends of the Picture Hse £3

Popcorn Cinema

Showcase

Junction 27 off M62, Batley
(01924) 420 622
Sun-Thu 11am-10pm, Fri-Sat 11am-late
Adults £5.70, Conc. £4

Ster Century

The Light, The Headrow 0870 240 3696
Sun-Thu 11am-10pm, Fri-Sat 11am-late
Adults £4.80-£5.80, NUS £3.80-£4.30,
Kids/OAPs £4.30

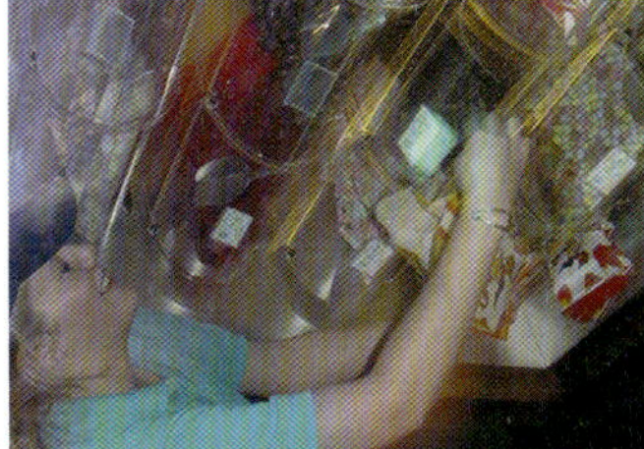

Vue

Cardigan Fields, Kirkstall Road
0871 240 240
Sun-Thu 12pm-9pm (last showing),
Fri 12pm-12am (last showing),
Sat 9.30am-12am (last showing)
Adults £4.80-£5.70, Kids £4.10,
OAPs £4.10

Comedy Venues

City Varieties

Swan Street (0113) 391 7777
One of the best-known variety venues in the country, this 18th century music hall has played host to comic legends like Ken Dodd, Ross Noble and, er... Keith Harris. The surroundings are suitably plush, but the lack of air conditioning can put a strain on your Mum roll-on. The shortsighted will appreciate the binoculars – perfect for honing in on Harry Hill's nose hair.
Various times and prices

HiFi Club

2 Central Road (0113) 242 7353
Jazz might not be a laughing matter, but the HiFi's Saturday night comedy session certainly is. Pulling in three top comics every week, crowds have been tickled of late with the likes of Rob Rouse and Toby Foster, with plenty of treats on the bill for 2005. Once your sides are crying out for the laughter to stop, join in with the club night, 'The Boogaloo Club', which follows the acts at 10pm. One of the most popular comedy nights in Leeds, and the dancing after sure beats that crappy disco at Jongleurs.
Sat 7pm-10pm (club night 10pm-3am)
£10/£9 members (£3 refund if not staying for club night)

Hyena Lounge Comedy Club

The Original Oak, 2 Otley Road
(0113) 275 1322
The Library, 229 Woodhouse Lane
(0113) 244 0794
The Queen's Arms, Harrogate Road,
Chapel Allerton (0113) 288 8165

Get your mitts on the itchy boxset

Get all 17 hot as hell titles for just £39 including postage and packaging

order at:

www.itchycity.co.uk/books
0113 246 0440

SO HOT... IT'S LIKE... SO HOT...

Bath Birmingham Brighton Bristol Cambridge Cardiff Cornwall Edinburgh Glasgow
Leeds Liverpool London Manchester Nottingham Oxford Sheffield York

The best in comedy that Leeds has to offer; it even saw off the likes of the short-lived Comedy Store with its pugil stick of talent and army of top bookings. Now with three venues to get all smug about, you'll get a selection of comics from the UK scene showing up every week and making the always up-for-it crowd choke on their cider with the hilarity of it all. The comics love it (possibly more than we do), you love it, and we'd gladly shave the word 'Hyena' into our pubic hair just to show how much we're fans of the whole operation. A fab atmosphere and an even fabber night.

Oak & Library: Thu 8pm (doors), 9pm (show), £5 (price includes free entry to following club night at The Library)
Queen's Arms: Last Fri of month 8pm (doors), 9pm (show), £7

Jongleurs
The Cube, Albion Street 0870 787 0707
Pretty much guaranteed top-notch acts with food at the table and a club night afterwards. Less a comedy club and more an overall 'night out'. Perfect for a stag/hen night. Not so perfect if you prefer to sit quietly in the corner on your own.
Thu-Sat from 8pm (dance-floor till 2pm)
From £8

Abbey House Museum
Abbey Walk, Kirkstall (0113) 230 5492
Old stuff. Bring your grandparents and pretend you've magically gone back in time... or something.
Tue-Fri/Sun 10am-5pm, Sat 12pm-5pm, closed Mon (last admissions 4pm)
Adults £3, Conc. £2, Kids £1

Leeds Industrial Museum
Armley Mills, Canal Road, Armley (0113) 263 7861
Once the world's largest woollen mill, now a museum Leeds schoolchildren are dragged to for GCSE history. A steam engine, a water wheel, and loads of facts about the clothing industry – all really useful in today's job market.
Tue-Sat 10am-5pm, Sun 1pm-5pm
Adults £2, Conc. £1, Kids 50p (accompanied by an adult)

Thackray Medical Museum
Beckett St (0113) 244 4343

This place got £3 million from a lottery grant. And what did they spend it on? A giant gut you can walk through. Cool. They also have the charmingly entitled exhibit, 'Pain, Pus, and Blood' and a look at medical advances through the ages.
Mon-Sun 10am-5pm (last entry 3pm)
Adults £4.90, Conc. £3.90, Kids £3.50,
Parking £1

Tropical World
Canal Gardens, Roundhay Park
(0113) 266 1850

As Carol Vordeman keeps telling us, it's good to sweat those toxins out. But if you'd rather not show off your bingo wings in the sauna, keep fully clothed and visit this set of greenhouses. As last night's cabernet sauvignon oozes from your pores watch butterflies, frut bats and meerkats attack bits of fruit. Which, by rights, should be your next step to a healthy new you.
Mon-Sun 10am-4pm (last admission 3.30pm)
Adults £3, Kids (8-15yrs) £2

Royal Armouries
Armouries Drive 08700 344 344

Discover 3000 years of history from the Dark Ages to present day. 8000 priceless artefacts can be found in five exquisite, themed galleries: War, Tournament, Self Defence, Hunting and Oriental. See history brought to life as interpreters describe accounts of people whose lives have been touched by the objects on display, then visit the museum shop for pocket money gifts and books, to replica swords and full armours. Museum entry is free so come on, what are you waiting for?
Mon-Sun 10am-5pm (closed 24th-25th Dec)
Free entry

Art Galleries

City Art Gallery
The Headrow (0113) 247 8248

Despite claiming to have "probably the best collection of 20th century art outside London", anyone who's visited the Tate Modern or Manchester City Art Gallery will find the collection pretty sparse. The Turner watercolours and drawings by Henry Moore

may be historically interesting, but the most eye-catching exhibits are the touring works. Mon-Sat 10am-5pm (Wed till 8pm), Sun
1pm-5pm
Free

Craft Centre & Design Gallery
City Art Gallery, The Headrow
(0113) 2478241
Gallery and shop showcasing contemporary designs in jewellery, glass, and ceramics. There are two major exhibitions per year, one around Christmas time – perfect for funny pots and plates for hard-to-buy-for relatives.
Tue-Fri 10am-5pm, Sat 10am-4pm
Free

Yorkshire Sculpture Park
West Bretton, Wakefield (01924) 832 631
If your walks in the park are spoilt by empty Coke cans and piles of dog poo, head here for 500 acres of landscaped wonderment. As well as the beauty of nature itself, you can weave your way through artworks by the likes of Barbara Hepworth, Henry Moore, and Elisabeth Frink, or browse the touring exhibitions in the Longside Gallery.

Apr-Nov: Grounds & centre 10am-6pm, indoor galleries 11am-5pm (Longside gallery till 4pm)
Nov-Apr: Grounds & centre 10am-5pm, indoor galleries 11am-4pm (Longside gallery till 3pm)
Parking £3 all day

Henry Moore Institute
74 The Headrow (0113) 234 3158

Permanent and touring exhibitions involving sculpture.
Mon-Sun 10am-5.30pm (Wed till 9pm)
Free

Headingley Cricket Ground
St Michael's Lane (0113) 278 7394
A disappointing, but undisastrous year for Yorkshire County Cricket Club – failing to make an impact on any of the domestic competitions, but by the same token, nothing horrific happened either – mainly because it's not logistically possible for them to be relegated again. However, a rejuvenated England side delivered a summer of

glory. Join the crowds in 2005 for an afternoon of fervent boozy support in the sun.
Tickets from £12

Leeds United

Elland Road (0113) 367 1166

After 2004, sales of tobacco and worry beads in West Yorkshire have probably never been higher. A disastrous campaign on the field, spectacularly high profile off the pitch woes, relegation, and mass player exodus, marked an all-time low for the club. Nonetheless, Leeds' legendary loyal following continue to turn out in their thousands to cheer on the Super Whites, still making Elland Road an intimidating venue for visiting Championship sides. Turn up here to witness Leeds' inevitable phoenix-esque rise back to the Premiership – well assuming the ground doesn't get turned into an ASDA first.
Tickets from £26

Leeds Rhinos

St Michael's Lane (0113) 278 6181

In sharp contrast to their flailing footballing brethren, the Rhinos continue to annihilate all before them. Last season's outstanding campaign, followed by victory over Bradford in the Super League final, realised an ambi-

tion that fans had been waiting 33 years for. Support for the team is excitable yet good natured, but if you're not prepared to take part in the south stand drinking games, you're the southern poof we always suspected you were.
Tickets from £12

Leeds Tykes

St Michael's Lane (0113) 278 6181

Still perennially in the shadow of their league counterparts, this union team continue to tick away in the Zurich Premiership. Mid-table mediocrity is the best that can be hoped for as the squad lacks the depth and resources to progress higher in the table, but is still likely to avoid relegation. Nonetheless it's still a fine place to cheer on the lads with a pint on a wintery afternoon.
Tickets from £10

Harewood House

Off A61 (Leeds-Harrogate Road)
(0113) 218 1010

Who'd have thought, in olden times it was actually ok to christen your son Capability? In fact, he could go on to have an important landscaping career, taming the grass of

noble types across the land. Don't believe us? Pay a visit to Harewood House and admire the green-fingered talents of Mr Brown. There's also a kid's playground, bird garden, and café designed by people with perfectly ordinary names.
Summer: Grounds & gardens 10am-6pm, House & terrace gallery 11am-4pm
Winter (weekends only): Grounds & gardens 10am-4pm, terrace gallery 11am-3.45pm
Freedom (house, grounds, gardens): Adult £10-£11, OAPs £8.25-£9.25, Kids/ NUS £5.50-£6
Bird garden & grounds only: Adult £7.25-£8.25, OAPs £6.25-£7.25, Kids/NUS £4.50-£5

Kirkstall Abbey

Abbey Walk, Abbey Road (0113) 230 5492
One of Britain's best preserved abbeys, founded in 1152 by a gang of Cistercian monks. Sexual deviants may like to know the car park opposite is allegedly a favourite spot for dogging.
Museum: Tue-Sat 10am-5pm, Sun 1pm-5pm; Adults £3, Conc. £2, Kids £1
Abbey site: dawn to dusk; Free

Meanwood Urban Valley Farm

Suger Well Road, Meanwood (0113) 262 9759
Chickens, pigs, and the obligatory crazy donkeys reside at this 14-acre working farm. Feel free to let the sheep nibble at your fingers, but do not, we repeat do not, go near Eeyore and his friends.
Mon-Sun 9am-4pm
Adults £1, Kids 50p, Under 12s free

Roundhay Park

Canal Gardens, Roundhay Park, Princes Avenue (0113) 266 1850

700 acres of trees, grass and squirrels. If you don't feel inspired by all the beautiful greenery you deserve to live out your days in a concrete block of flats with a lift that smells of wee.
Free

Temple Newsham House & Gardens

Temple Newsham (0113) 264 7321
17th century stately home with landscaped grounds by Capability Brown. Used to be the site of the Carling Leeds Festival, but they've obviously had enough of teenage moshers burning plastic carriers on their field, so it's now held at Braham Park.
House: Tue-Sun 1pm-5pm (Nov-Mar w/e only)
Home Farm: 10am-4pm,
Gardens: 10am-dusk, Estate: dusk-dawn
Adults £2, Kids 50p

itchycities...
Glasgow
Edinburgh
Leeds
York
Manchester
Liverpool
Sheffield
Nottingham
Birmingham
Cambridge
Cardiff
Oxford
Bristol
London
Brighton
Bath
and now
introducing...
itchy Cornwall
CORNWALL
www.itchycity.co.uk

The Town Hall
The Headrow (0113) 224 3801

Does what you'd expect of a hall in a city that's called town. Keep your eyes peeled for the occasional 'rave' or new age event, complete with women waving rainbows about and skin-heads burning bonfires or something.

Out of Leeds

Harrogate

It's the law in Yorkshire that every day you have to eat at least one scone. Join the pastry pilgrimage at the Harrogate branch of Betty's Tearooms (1 Parliament Street). After you've licked all that cream off your fingers, where better to detox than the Turkish Baths and Health Spa (Parliament Street – 01423 556 746)? If you're more into brain than brawn, catch a show at the Harrogate Theatre (01423 502 116), or show your knowledge of world cuisine at one of the town's many fine restaurants – try Attic (62 Union Street – 01423 524 400) or Rajput (01423 562 113). Since the Lib Dems got kicked out in the last bi-election, you can no longer delight in their annual party conference, but the annual Harrogate In Bloom festival should be enough to raise a tender and feeble smile.

Ilkley

An ideal base for exploring the moors, this well-to-do spa town has a staggering number of charity shops to browse through should walking bring you out in hives. Also home to a branch of Betty's – the olde worlde tea shop that sees OAPs queuing round the block for a chocolate éclair served on a doily. Lovely – retire here today.

Lightwater Valley
North Stainley, Ripon (01765) 635 368

Ok, so it's no Alton Towers (hell, it's not even Blackpool Pleasure Beach), but this family theme park is still a handy place to entertain the youngsters/spend an ironic student day out. Scoff at the Swan Lake pedal boats before wetting your pants on the wooden rollercoaster.

May-Oct 10am-4.30pm (Rides open at 10.30am, days very – call to check)
Over 1.2m height £14.50, Under 1.2m £13, Under 1m free, OAPs/Disabled £6.95

National Museum of Photography, Film & Television
Pictureville, Bradford 0870 7010 200

To answer Homer Simpson's question – "How can one little insulated wire bring so much happiness?" – the NMPFT reveals the wondrous world of film, photography, and the goggle box. With over three million items on display, you can chart television's history from the world's first footage to the latest in IMAX technology. It's a beautiful, beautiful thing.

Tue-Sun 10am-6pm, closed Mon
Cinemas: Mon-Sun 10am-late
Free (charges for cinema screenings and special exhibitions)

Salts Mill
Shipley, Saltaire 01274 531 185

Built by local philanthropist Titus Salt in 1853, this textile mill now houses three public floors of art and crafts, including a selection of work by David Hockney. After browsing the staggering selection of art and design books, consider starting your own installation over Thai chicken pancakes at the Salts Diner, or something seafaring in the top floor fish restaurant.

Mon-Fri 10am-5.30pm,
Sat-Sun 10am-6pm
Free

Scarborough

About an hour and a half away, Scabs is your traditional British seaside resort. Not as glitzy as Blackpool, colder than Margate, but less awful than Skegness, you can stuff your gob with fish and chips before shovelling a tenner's worth of 2ps into a penny arcade machine for a ceramic donkey/Spice Girls keychain. Check out the annual 'Beached' music festival for some local live music.

Whitby

Most famous for Dracula's steps, fish and chips, and not being quite as good as Scarborough. Nonetheless it still draws two diametrically opposed sectors of the community – American tourists and Goths.

York

Once the capital of England, York stays true to its Viking roots with more pubs than actual residents (not really, but almost). As well as being a stunning example of Gothic architecture, the York Minster, and its towering spire, is a handy navigational point when the local brews have skewered your directional skills. Grab a copy if itchy York for a pocket-sized guide to the city's charms.

Yorkshire Dales

Recreate your favourite Emmerdale scene – be it lesbian tryst, death by pub wall, or hunt for Inca treasure – amidst the breathtaking scenery of the North York Moors National Park. As well as unlimited am-dram options, highlights include the Black Sheep Brewery in Masham, and Wetwang – home to Countdown anchorman and sartorial style leader Richard Whitely.

Citrus

13a North Lane (0113) 274 9002
The best pool in Headingley.
Mon-Sun 12pm-11.30pm
£7/hour

The Elbow Room

64 Call Lane (0113) 245 7011
Forget old men with varnished cues, padded gloves, and personally inscribed pool chalk – this is the coolest place to sink some balls in the city. Spread over two floors, with 15 SAM American pool tables, even if you suck at the good ol' game, there's, big screens and burgers to keep you occupied.
Mon-Thu 12pm-2am, Fri-Sat 12pm-3am, Sun 12pm-12am
Sun-Mon £5 p/hr all day, Tue-Sat before 7pm £5 p/hr, after 7pm £8 p/hr

Northern Snooker Centre

Kirkstall Road (0113) 243 3015
Mon-Sun 9am-7am (open 22 hours), Bar 12pm-1am
Pool £5.49 p/hr, Snooker £4.68 p/hr
Membership £6 p/yr

Riley's Pool & Snooker Club

1 Cross Belgrave Street (0113) 243 3391
Mon-Sun 12am-12am (24 hours)
Pool £6.25 p/hr, Snooker £4.25 p/hr

Bowling

AMF Bowling

Merrion Centre, Merrion Way
0845 658 1271
Sun-Fri 9.30am-12am,
Sat 9.30am-12.30am
Adults £2.80-£3.70 p/game,
Kids £2.35-£2.90, Shoe hire £1

Hollywood Bowl

Cardigan Fields Road, Kirkstall Road
(0113) 279 9111
Mon-Sun 10am-12am
Adults from £2.60, Kids from £1.80

Karting, Paintball & Laser

Paintball Commando

0808 108 9831
Call to arrange times
£15 (incl. equipment, 50 balls, lunch/
refreshments)

F1 Racing

Pepsi Max Raceway, Kathryn Avenue,
Huntington, York (01904) 673555
Mon-Fri 11am-7pm, Sat-Sun 10am-7pm
From £9.50

Pole Position Indoor Karting

Sayner Lane 0845 1260613
Mon-sun 10am-10pm
30mins £20 per driver

Casinos

It's free to join all the casinos below, but you'll have to wait 24hours between joining and your first visit.

Gala Casino

Wellington Bridge Street, Westgate
(0113) 389 3700
Sun-Fri 2pm-6am, Sat 6pm-4am

Grosvenor Casino

Moortown Corner House, 343 Harrogate
Road (0113) 269 5051
Sun-Fri 6pm-6am, Sat 6pm-4am

Napoleon Casino

Bingley Street (0113) 244 5393
Sun-Fri 2pm-5am, Sat 2pm-4am

Strip Clubs

All the clubs below have a smart/casual dress code, so leave the trainers/Kappa tracksuit at home.

Blue Leopard

36 Wellington Street (0113) 245 5103
Mon-Thu 8pm-2.30am, Fri 8pm-4am,
Sat 6pm-4am, Sun 8pm-1am
Entry £10, Dance £10

DV8

9 Briggate (0113) 243 4293
Mon-Sat 5pm-2am
Entry £10, Dance £10

Purple Door

5 York Place (0113) 245 0556
Mon-Thu 8pm-2am, Fri-Sat 6pm-4am
Entry £10, Dance £10

Property Developers

Barratt Homes
14 Royds Hall Road, Pavillion Business Park (0113) 279 0099
www.barratthomes.co.uk

Bryant Homes
3300 Century Way, Thorpe Park (0113) 232 1400
www.bryant.co.uk

Cala Homes
Victoria House, Lawnswood Business Park (0113) 239 9500
www.cala.co.uk

Crosby Homes
Morwick Hall, Mortec Park, York Road (0113) 265 2000
www.crosbyhomes.co.uk

KW Linfoot
Whitehall Waterfront, 2 Riverside Way (0113) 391 6300
www.kwlinfootplc.com

Persimmon Homes
3 Hepton Court, York Road (0113) 240 9726
www.persimmonhomes.com

Letting Agents

Headingley Lets
City centre rentals: Hunslet Road (0113) 225 1313
Student rentals: 6 Headingley Lane (0113) 225 1717
Suburban rentals: 81-83 Otley Road

(0113) 225 1616
www.headingley.uk.net

Jump

75 Town Street, Armley (0113) 290 7900
Also branches in Pudsey, Bramley, Chapel Allerton, Garforth, Harehills, North Leeds and South Leeds
www.jumpnow.co.uk

LS1 City Apartments

2 Cherry Tree Walk (0113) 234 4111
www.ls-1.co.uk

Manning Stainton

20 Otley Road (0113) 274 8646
Also branches in Guiseley, Horsforth, Wortley, Morley, Rothwell and Chapel Allerton
www.manningstainton.co.uk

Morgans

20 Otley Road, Headingley
(0113) 2179 090
www.cityliving.co.uk

Parklane Properties

25-27 Otley Road, Headingley
(0113) 230 4949
172-174 Harrogate Road, Chapel Allerton
(0113) 237 0000
www.parklaneproperties.com
One of Leeds' premier letting and property management companies, Parklane has two branches in Leeds covering letting and selling, with their Headingley branch catering for student tenants and the Chapel Allerton location geared more towards professional rentals and sales. With a reputation built on dedication to quality and the ability to deal with each and every property sale or purchase with energy and determination, they're always a popular choice. And with friendly staff ready to give advice and tenants guide's to take home with you, the only scary bit is forking out the money.
Otley Rd: Mon-Fri 9am-5.30pm,
Sat 10am-4pm, Sun closed
Harrogate Rd: Mon-Fri 9am-6pm,
Sat 9am-4pm, Sun closed

Residential Sales

Alan Cooke

15a Stonegate Road (0113) 289 9669
382 Harrogate Road, Moortown
(0113) 288 8666
www.alan-cooke.co.uk

Carter Jonas

7-8 Park Place (0113) 242 5155
www.carterjonas.co.uk

Castlehill

21 Otley Road (0113) 278 7427
www.castlehill.co.uk

Hendys

116-118, Harrogate Road, Chapel Allerton (0113) 268 2100

Hunters

15 Park Place (0113) 218 2446
www.huntersnet.co.uk

Jump

75 Town street (0113) 290 7900
www.jumpnow.co.uk

LS1

2 Cherry Tree Walk (0113) 234 4111
18 Park Row, Leeds (0113) 200 6350
www.ls-1.co.uk

Parklane Properties

172-174 Harrogate Road, Chapel Allerton (0113) 237 0000
www.parklaneproperties.com

Trusted, experienced and innovative property company, with friendly and approachable staff who are always ready to give advice and help take the stress out of buying or selling a home. With one of the most up-to-date property websites in Leeds under their belt, and willingness to help you through the process every step of the way (from viewings to handing over the keys), finding your ideal home will be a doddle. Just don't forget to invite them to your house-warming party.
Mon-Fri 9am-6pm, Sat 9am-4pm, Sun closed

Pickerings

16 St. Annes Road, Headingley (0113) 274 6746

Morgans

32 Park Place (0113) 398 0099
www.cityliving.co.uk

Furnishings & Interiors

Domane Interiors

5 Bridge Street (0113) 245 0701

Futon Company

30-32 Woodhouse Lane (0113) 2450770

Habitat

West Yorkshire Retail Park (01924) 477081

Ikea

West Yorkshire Retail Park (01924) 423296

Loft

24 Dock Street (0113) 305 1515

Peter Maturi

84-86 Vicar Lane (0113) 245 3887

Robert Mason

70 North Street (0113) 242 2434

West Park Interiors

Lower Blayds Court, 20 Swinegate (0113) 245 4522

parklane 
parklane
because you
want more.
STUDENTS:
25-27 Otley Road, Headingley, Leeds LS6 3AA 0113 230 4949
SALES AND PROFESSIONALS:
172-174 Harrogate Road, Chapel Allerton, Leeds LS7 4NZ 0113 237 0000
www.parklaneproperties.com

body

Box Creative Hairdressing

3 Lower Briggate (0113) 245 6869

Sometimes a simple decision can be very costly, and if you make the mistake of entrusting a clown brandishing a pair of scissors with your barnet, you deserve everything you get. The folk at Box will treat your hair like spun gold and coif and tease it into any cutting-edge, trendy style you so choose. Specialising in bold colours and styles for those willing to experiment, the staff are friendly and willing to listen to you babble on for an hour about your unruly fringe. Restyles and conditioning treatments mean you can have a proper pampering session, and a central location means even your feet will leave with a smile.

Mon-Wed/Fri-Sat 10am-6pm,
Thu 10am-7pm; Men £19.50, Women
£29.50, NUS 50% discount Mon-Wed

Expo

White Cloth Hall, Crown Street
(0113) 234 7235

City centre salon next to the Corn Exchange offering cuts, colours and treatments in a stylish setting. As well as having the expertise to transform your barnet from a Kenny Rogers to a Kirsten Dunst, they're renowned

for their revitalising head massages administered during the conditioning stage – sink back into your chair and feel your eyes droop with the sheer relaxation of it all. Tigi and Phytologie product ranges mean you've got some goodies to take home too, to keep that 'do' looking top notch.
Mon-Wed/Fri 9am-6pm, Thu 9am-7pm, Sat 9am-5pm; Men £29, Women from £31

Toni & Guy

Boar Lane (0113) 234 4334
22 King Edward Street (0113) 244 9610
Renowned national chain.
Mon-Tue 9am-5.15pm, Wed-Thu 9am-6.45pm, Fri 9am-6pm, Sat 9am-5.15pm Men from £30, Women from £37

Afro/Mixed Hairdressers

The Barber Shop

85 Kirkgate (0113) 246 7587
A down-to-earth city centre barbers with their fingers (or er, scissors) firmly on the style pulse. Specialising in funky hair tattoos (patterns and designs shaved into the hair or eyebrows), they also offer a complete range of traditional and modern services including wet shaves (Sweeny Todd style), cutting, highlights, fades and flat tops. A

great spot for afro, European and mixed hair textures, piercing and manicures are also available. Ladies on request.
Mon-Thu/Sat 8.30am-5pm, Fri 8.30am-6pm Haircuts from £5, hair tattoos from £15, saves from £7

Relaxation & Beauty

Hanalee

Garden Unit, The Light, The Headrow (0113) 244 9898
Swanky new beauty salon that'll happily give you a top-to-toe makeover. Plonk yourself on a fluffy stool for hair design, make-up recommendations, colour analysis or a wardrobe and image consultation. Crikey.
Mon-Wed/Sat 9am-6pm, Thu 9am-late, Fri 9am-7pm, Sun 11am-5pm Manicure £15

Skingenesis

2nd Floor, Duncan House,
14-16 Duncan Street (0113) 244 8999

Non-surgical, non-invasive, 'walk-in-walk-out' treatments to combat ageing skin, acne scarring, scars, stretch marks and cellulite.
Call in for a free consultation

U4EA

35 Arndale Centre, Otley Road
(0113) 230 7505

If the Otley Run has left you riddled with toxins, impurities and strange aches and pains, escape to this tranquil Headingley spot to reclaim your inner balance. Offering alternative therapies and handmade organic products, the friendly team will soothe your body and mind with everything from aromatherapy massage, shiatsu, and reiki, to reflexology, facials, and hopi ear candles.

Owner Maria is also on hand for down-to-earth advice and cheery chatter. Absolutely recommended.
Mon 12pm-6pm, Tue-Fri 10am-6pm, Sat 9am-5pm (occasional Sun and Mon-Fri 6pm-9pm for bookings only)
Aromatherapy half massage with consultation (45mins) £22.50, thereafter £17.50 per session (30mins)

Esporta

The Light, The Headrow (0113) 233 7500

'Fitness arena', separate free weights area, pool, relaxation room, steam, sauna and spa pools, sunbeds, health and beauty salon, aerobics studio, and café/bar
Mon-Fri 6am-10pm, Sat 9am-7pm, Sun 10am-7pm

Membership discussed after consultation

LA Fitness

6-24 Albion Street 0870 163 2047

Gym, pool, personal assessments, sauna, spa, steam room, beauty treatments and café/bar
Mon-Thu 6.30am-10pm, Fri 6.30am-8pm, Sat-Sun 9am-5pm
Membership discussed after consultation

Living Well

Hilton, Neville Street (0113) 244 5443

Gym, pool, spa, sauna, steam room
Mon-fri 6.30am-10pm, Sat-Sun 9am-5pm
Membership £49 p/month, joining fee £29

Virgin Active Life Centre

Cardigan Fields, Kirkstall 0845 130 1555

Pool, solarium, sauna, studios, 12,000 sq ft gym with TVs and dedicated women's-only bit, crèche, and café/bar
Mon-Fri 6am-12am, Sat-Sun 8am-9pm
Membership £49 per month (£38 off peak), Joining fee £50

Tattoo Parlours/Piercing

Ultimate Skin Tattoo

29a New Briggate (0113) 244 4940

With a team from all corners of the globe, you'll be party to a whole world of tattooing knowledge if you choose to get needled here. Friendly staff, clean premises and the skills to produce as big a tattoo as you can stand, you can also get pierced at the same time. And if you fancy getting tatted in the sun, they also offer tattooing holidays – ace.

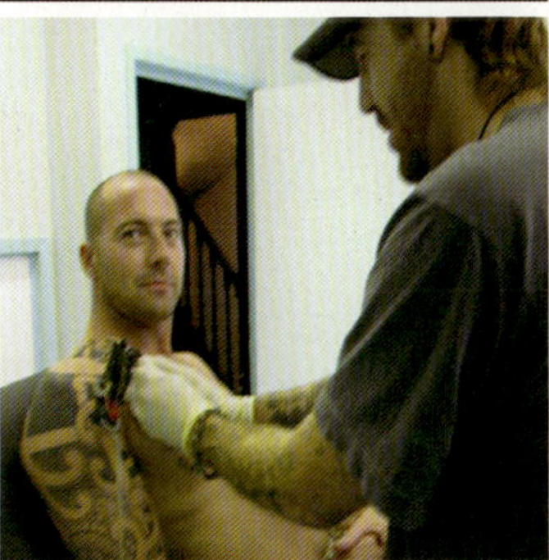

www.ultimateskintattoo.com
Mon-Sun 12pm-8pm
Tattoos from £25, piercing from £15

laters

Late Night Drinking

Call Lane is a late-night drinking Mecca, with The Elbow Rooms – (0113) 245 7011, Normans – (0113) 234 3988, and Revolution – (0113) 243 2778 all open till 2am Mon-Sat.

Cigarettes at 4am?

The Tong Road Total garage – (0113) 220 5310 is open right round the clock, as is the garage on Cardigan Road. GimmeSomeBeer – 0845 6444 888 – will happily deliver cigs and booze to your home till 5am Sun-Thu, and till 6am Fri-Sat.

After Hours Fridge Stocking

Tesco, Roundhay Road, Roundhay 0845 677 9414, and Asda, Owlcotes Centre, Pudsey 0113 236 1222, are open 24hrs for those of you who like to push their trolley in peace/are prone to the occasional late night craving.

Food Now!

For post-pub munchies, Lucky's in Hyde Park delivers pizzas and kebabs until 3am, while Fortune Cookie delivers Oriental fodder till 2am.

Nice Food Now!

Decent food is hard to find at three in the morning – but if beans on toast just won't cut it – try this lot. Naffee's in Hyde Park and Tariq's in Headingley will dish you up Indian delights until 3am Fri-Sat. Or try Fred's (1 Crown Street – 0113 234 1999) who'll supply you with a hot slice of pizza till 1am.

Post Club Action/ All-Nighters

If you're determined to wear holes in your soles, pop along to Glass House at Mission, which runs from 2.30am-9pm Sat night/ Sun morning once a month. It's the official Federation after-party, so expect misbehaviour. After that, you'll just have to settle with the Hollyoaks omnibus – joy!

Café Society

Starbucks at Borders, Briggate – (0113) 242 4400, is open till 9pm Mon-Sat. For a taste of Morocco, try L'Oranaise Café on Hyde Park Corner, which serves after 11pm on Fri-Sat nights.

Late Night Shopping

Shopping in your lunch hour is awfully organised of you, but why not make the most of Leeds Alive After 5 and concentrate on your BLT instead? Many city centre retailers including Harvey Nics, TopShop, Debenhams, H&M, Miss Selfridge, Schuh, Next and The Victoria Quarter stay open late (7pm) Thu-Sat, and more retailers are to follow. Persuading us to indulge in more shopping? Now that's more like it.

After Work Beauty Fix

Most salons have late night opening on Thursdays, including Box Creative and Expo, who both run appointments until around 6pm. Hanalee at The Light opens till 8pm on Thu and 7pm on Fri.

Late Night Culture

Check out the exciting array of art on show at the City Gallery, which is now open till 8pm on Wed, or the adjacent Henry Moore Institute which closes at 9pm. For nocturnal film-buffs, The Ster Century Cinema has late night showings at the weekend.

Other Places

Shoot pool until 7am at Northern Snooker in Kirkstall, or gamble your fortune away at

Gala, Grosvenor or Napoleon Casinos until 4am. If it's getting late and you still haven't pulled, head to the Blue Leopard where a bevy of beauties will shake, shake, wiggle, wiggle until 4am Fri-Sat.

All prices are per room per night, and based on standard double rooms, unless otherwise stated

42 The Calls

42 The Calls (0113) 244 0099
Townhouse hotel overlooking the river Aire. Has its own award-winning restaurant.
Study room £130, Double deluxe standard £170, ask for special w/e rates

Crowne Plaza

Wellington Street (0113) 244 2200
Forget the fully equipped gym and head instead for the beauty services. Finish off watching an in-room movie in a fluffy bath-robe. Bliss.
£80-£150 week, £150-£210 weekend

Hilton

Neville Street (0113) 244 2000
There may be no Paris, but there's plenty of a la carte cuisine in their in-house restaurant.
£95-£105 week, £84 weekend (includes breakfast at w/e)

Malmaison

Sovereign Quay (0113) 398 1000
Stylish hotel near the train station. Rooms boast big beds, CD players, and cable TV. There's also a gym, but we didn't think you'd be interested in that.
£129 week, £99 weekend

Leeds Marriott

**4 Trevelyan Square,
Boar Lane (0113) 236 6366**
Has an indoor pool, spa, sauna and steam-

accommodation

Get the best rates online.

Guaranteed.
www.parkplazaleeds.com

Park Plaza Leeds
Boar Lane, City Square
Leeds LS1 5NS United Kingdom

T: +44 (0) 113 380 4000
pplinfo@parkplazahotels.co.uk
www.parkplaza.com

AMSTERDAM • ANTWERP • BELFAST • BERLIN • BUDAPEST • CARDIFF
DRESDEN • EINDHOVEN • JERUSALEM • JOHANNESBURG • LEEDS
LONDON • NAHARIYA • NOTTINGHAM TEL AVIV • TRIER • UTRECHT AND
MANY OTHER WORLDWIDE KEY LOCATIONS

room. Unfortunately, it also has an additional charge for breakfast.
Approx. £140

Novotel

4 Whitehall, Whitehall Quay (0113)
Two minutes from the rail station, so great for spotters.
£50-£132

Park Plaza Leeds

City Square, Boar Lane (0113) 380 4000
You just don't get more central than this. A pedestrian crossing away from city station, this 4-star, 187-roomed, design-led hotel offers fab views of the city as well as all of the facilities you'd expect, including air conditioning, high speed Internet access and a fully fitted gym. With a ground floor bar perfect for starting off a night and Far

East fusion restaurant Chino Latino providing a stunning menu of eastern flavours and Japanese cuisine, this is the only square of Leeds you'll need to know about.
W/day and w/end prices include breakfast, call for the best rates

Queens Hotel

City Square (0113) 243 1323

Landmark hotel adjoining the train station. Overlooks City Square so is great for eyeing Saturday night's Majestyks queue. Has almost completed a £8 million (count 'em) refurbishment.

£90-£185 week (room only), £75 weekend (includes b/fast)

Radisson SAS

The Light, The Headrow (0113) 236 6000

Swanky city centre hotel housed in The Light development. Has a 1920s-inspired bar as well as rooms in Art Deco, Hi-Tech and Italian styles.

Single £129-£154 week,
£90-£125 weekend (both include breakfast)
Double rooms £10 extra

Quebecs

9 Quebec Street (0113) 244 8989

Beautiful Victorian boutique hotel in the former Leeds & Count Liberal Club.

Town house £125, Town house club £135,
Weekend rates from £80

Bewley's Hotel Leeds

City Walk, Sweet Street (0113) 234 2340

It's only £69 a room, but Bewley's is better equipped and nicer than most hotels that charge twice that. Posh rooms, with free Internet access and all the gizmos you'd expect from a four star hotel. Throw in a top notch brasserie, parking and perfect location, (two minutes walk from the city centre and two minutes drive from the motorways), and it wins itchy's best of the beds 2005.

Doubles £69

Holiday Inn Express

Cavendish Street (0113) 242 6200

About a mile from the city centre, and popular with briefcase-wielding types. Prices include continental breakfast.

Double/twin £69 (£59-£69 at w/e)

Golden Lion

2 Briggate (0113) 243 6454

Just round the corner from Call Lane, this reliable hotel is stumbling distance from the city's nightlife.

Single £90, Twin £99, Deluxe single £105,
Deluxe twin £115

THINK YOU'RE A BIT FLASH AT PHOTOGRAPHY?

THINK YOU CAN DO BETTER THAN THIS LOT?

To be honest, we'd hope so.

We're always on the lookout for photographers, and looking at these abysmal efforts (no names...), it's easy to understand why.

Drop us a line at
artwork@itchymedia.co.uk

Sleep Inn

97-107 Vicar Lane (0113) 243 6810
£59 week & weekend

Travel Inn

Wellington Street (0113) 242 8105
Next to T.G.I Friday's, should you feel like taking a week off and working your way through the whole menu.
Mon-Thu £56.95 per room,
Fri-Sun £52.95 per room

Budget

Butlers Hotel

40 Cardigan Road (0113) 274 4755
Overlooks the cricket ground, but if the thought of men in white wool sends you to sleep, they also have satellite TV.
Rooms from £40

Clock Hotel

317 Roundhay Road (0113) 249 0304
£45 week, £50 weekend

Hotel Budapest

12-14 Cardigan Road (0113) 275 2034
£50 (£62 en-suite) week, £46 (£55 en-suite)
Breakfast included

Manxdene Hotel

154 Woodsley Road (0113) 243 2586
£40 week (£50 en-suite), £35 weekend (£45 en-suite)
All prices include breakfast

St Michael's Tower Hotel

5 St Michael's Villas, Cardigan Road (0113) 275 5557
Rooms from £48
Breakfast included

useful info

travel/useful info

Taxis

City Cabs .... (0113) 246 9999
Streamline .... (0113) 244 3322
Telecabs .... (0113) 263 7777

Private Hire

Amber .... (0113) 263 6445
Arrow .... (0113) 258 2573
Furlongs .... (0113) 226 7000
Parkways .... (0113) 274 4441
Pegasus .... (0113) 279 9999
Premier .... (0113) 288 8333
Point to Point .... (0113) 236 0860
Star .... (0113) 249 0099
Top Line .... (0113) 274 1000
Wheels .... (0113) 248 1111

Bus Companies

Black Prince (local) .... (0113) 252 6033
First Leeds (local) .... (0113) 381 5550
Metroline (local bus/train info)...................
.... (0113) 245 7676
National Express (booking line) ....
.... 08705 80 80 80
Yorkshire Coastliner .... (0113) 244 8976

Train Companies

GNER (Telesales) 08457 225 225
Metroline (local train/bus info) ....
.... (0113) 245 7676
Midland Mainline 08457 125 678
Northern Trains (prev. Arriva) ....
.... 0870 602 3322

National Rail Enquiries 08457 48 49 50
Virgin Trains (Customer Services) ....
....0870 789 1234

Airports

Leeds Bradford ....(0113) 250 9696
Manchester ....(0161) 489 3000

Tourist Info

Leeds City Station Branch ....
....(0113) 242 5242

Travel Agents

STA
Leeds University S.U. ....(0113) 245 9400
88 Vicar Lane 0870 168 6878
182 Woodhouse Lane ......(0113) 245 8440
National Telesales 08701 600 599
(Mon-Wed 9am-8pm, Thu-Fri 9am-7pm,
Sat 10am-8pm, Sun 11am-5pm)

Health, Advice & Emergencies

British Gas 0845 609 1122
Childline ....(0113) 244 4004
City Council ....(0113) 234 8080
Hertz Rent-A-Car 0870 846 0014
Leeds General Infirmary .(0113) 243 2799
NHS Direct 0845 46 47 48
National Lock & Safe (24hr) ....
....0800 0853 697
Nightline (listening) ....(0113) 380 1381
Police (Non Emergency) 0845 606 0606
Rape & Abuse Line 0808 8000 123
RSPCA ....(0113) 245 5132
Samaritans ....(0113) 245 6789
Yorkshire Water Helpline ..0845 124 24 24

takeaway

Tell your mates from down south the price of a margherita from a Leeds pizza joint and they'll gasp in wonder. Explain that this price is for a large and includes delivery and their eyes will narrow in undisguised envy. But who cares if your friends hate you when takeaway is this cheap? Leeds delivers pizzas, curries, and all kinds of burgers cheap as chips. And your mates don't want to know how cheap chips are...

Pizzas/Burgers

Big Mamas
25 North Lane, Headingley
(0113) 274 4899
Delivers
Mon-Sat 5pm-2am

Caesars
209 Stanningley Road (0113) 279 8888
Delivers
Mon-Sun 5pm-12.30am

Domino's Pizza
12 St Anne's Road, Headingley
(0113) 2899 559
Delivers
Mon-Thu 4pm-11pm,
Fri-Sun 12pm-11pm

Harpos
23 Otley Road (0113) 278 2415
Delivers
Mon-Sun 5pm-12am

Italiano Pizza
109 Chapelton Road (0113) 239 2939
Delivers
Mon-Sun 5pm-late

Luckys
81 Raglan Road 0500 11 33 45
Delivers
Mon-Sat 5pm-3am, Sun 5pm-1am

Milanos
79 Raglan Road (0113) 242 5954
Delivers
Mon-Sat 5pm-3am, Sun 5pm-1am

Fish & Chips

Bretts Fish Restaurant
14 North Lane, Headingley
(0113) 232 3344
No delivery, but eat-in restaurant as well as takeaway
Restaurant: Tue-Fri 12pm-2pm/5pm-9pm,
Sat 11.30am-9.30pm, Sun 12.30pm-7pm
Takeaway: Mon-Sun 11.30am-10pm

Bryan's
9 Weetwood Lane (0113) 278 5679
No delivery, but eat-in restaurant as well as takeaway
Restaurant: Mon-Fri 12pm-10pm,
Sat-Sun 12pm-10pm
Takeaway: Mon-Wed 12pm-2pm/4.30pm-
10pm, Thu-Sun 12pm-10.30pm

Chinese/Pacific Rim

Fortune Cookie
81 Raglan Road Hyde Park
08000 155 444
Delivers
Mon-Sat 5pm-3am, Sun 5pm-1am

www.itchycity.co.uk

Norman

36 Call Lane (0113) 234 3988
Pacific Rim noodles and rice in front of your
own TV. No delivery, pick up only.
Mon-Sun 12pm-7.30pm

Sakura

21 North Lane, Headingley
(0113) 224 2323
Delivers
Mon-Sun 5pm-12am

Indian

Nafees

69a Raglan Road (0113) 245 3128
No delivery
Mon-Sun 12pm-3am

Nazamz

201 Woodhouse Street (0113) 243 8515
Delivers
Mon-Fri 5pm-1am, Sat-Sun 5pm-2.30am

Sultans

39 New Briggate (0113) 243 8500
Delivers after 6pm
Mon-Sat 11am-4am, Sun 2pm-12am

Clarendon Wa
A
B
Leeds Met. Uni.
C
D
Woodhouse Lane
1
A58 (M)
P
Portland
Portland Crescent
P
Cookridge Street
Millennium Square
Joseph's Well
Nelson Mandella Gardens
Calverley Street
2
P
Park Street
Oxford Row
Town Hall
Library
The Light
Westgate
The Headr
3
International Pool
Park Square East
Cross Street
S Parade
East Parade
S Parade
Park Square West
Greek St
Little Queen Street
St Paul's Street
Park Row
4
P
Queen Street
Park Place
Parade Wk
Bond S
KIRKSTALL RD + LEISURE PARK
Back York Pl
York Pl
Quebec Street
City Square
Wellington Street
5
Aire Street
Bo
Whitehall Road
P
River Aire
P
Leeds Rail Station
6
Neville St

E
F
G
H
Grosvenor Casino
Merrion Way
A64 (M)
Byron Street
errion entre
Belgrave St
Nile St
Trafalgar Street
Gower St
Regent Street
Merrion Street
New Briggate
The Grand Theatre
Templer Street
St John's Centre
Mint Club
Eastgate
City Varieties
Lady Lane
Lands Lane
Victoria
Quarter
Union Street
West Yorkshire Playhouse
bion Place
Harvey Nichols
Vicar Lane
George Street
ommercial St.
Briggate
Bus Station
New York St
York Street
HiFi Club
Kirkgate
Duncan St
Corn Exchange
Royal Armouries
Call Lane
The Calls
Leeds City Centre
P
Golden Lion Hotel
inegate
TO M62, M1
ELLAND ROAD

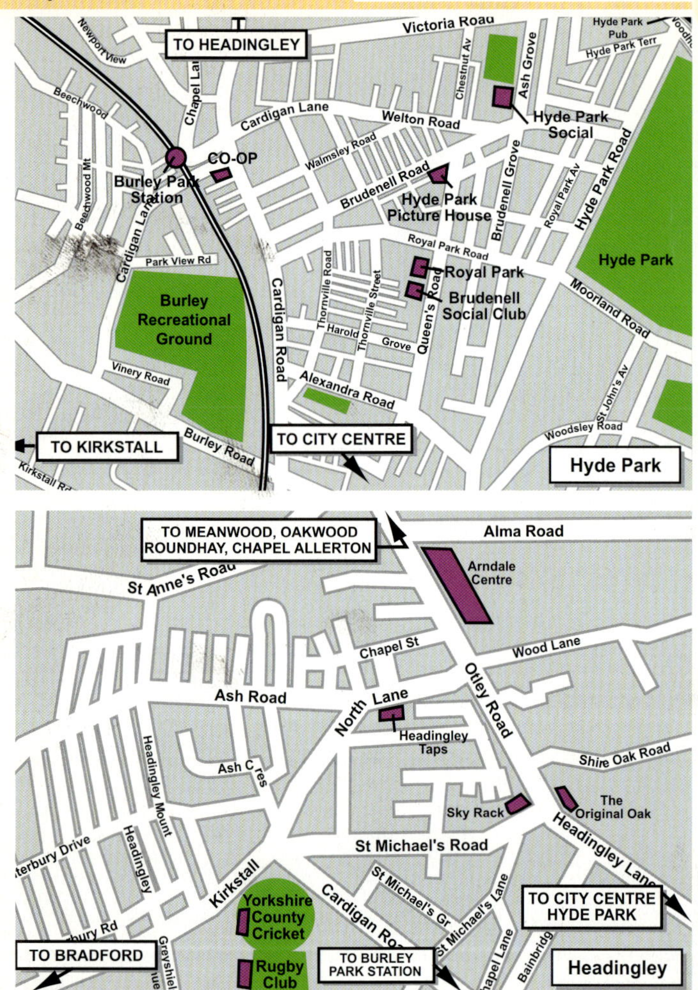
TO HEADINGLEY
Victoria Road
Hyde Park Pub
Hyde Park Terr
Newport View
Beechwood
Beechwood Mt
Chapel Lane
Cardigan Lane
Cardigan Lane
Chestnut Av
Ash Grove
Welton Road
Hyde Park Social
Burley Park Station
CO-OP
Walmsley Road
Brudenell Road
Brudenell Grove
Royal Park Av
Hyde Park Road
Park View Rd
Hyde Park Picture House
Royal Park Road
Royal Park
Brudenell Social Club
Hyde Park
Burley Recreational Ground
Thornville Road
Thornville Street
Thornville Grove
Harold Road
Queen's Road
Moorland Road
Cardigan Road
Vinery Road
Alexandra Road
St John's Av
Woodsley Road
TO KIRKSTALL
Kirkstall Rd
Burley Road
TO CITY CENTRE
Hyde Park
TO MEANWOOD, OAKWOOD
ROUNDHAY, CHAPEL ALLERTON
Alma Road
Arndale Centre
St Anne's Road
Chapel St
Wood Lane
Ash Road
North Lane
Otley Road
Headingley Taps
Headingley Mount
Ash Cres
Shire Oak Road
The Original Oak
Sky Rack
Headingley Lane
terbury Drive
Headingley
St Michael's Road
St Michael's Gr
St Michael's Lane
Chapel Lane
Bainbridg
TO CITY CENTRE
HYDE PARK
Kirkstall
Yorkshire County Cricket
Cardigan Rd
Greyshiel
TO BRADFORD
terbury Rd
Rugby Club
TO BURLEY PARK STATION
Headingley

leeds 2005

www.itchyleeds.co.uk

Editorial
City Editors - Andy Germaine, Ben Johnson
Editor-In-Chief - Gayle Hetherington
Assistant Editor - Kim Whatley

Contributors - Dan Benton, Natasha Browne, Jamie Cohen, Hazel Davis, John Emmerson, Adam Johnstone, Peter Lewis, Scott Oxley, Emma Parker, Luke-Joseph Putres, David Strinati, Arindam Rej

Design
Chris McNamara
Erlend Sakshaug
Matt Wood
Nick Edwards

Main Photography
David Bussian @ pcb grace photography - www.pcbgrace.com

Photography
Emanuela Evangelisti, Paul Heany, Becky Moore, Olivia Nunn, Chris McNamara, Linda Shakesby

Team itchy
Commercial - Andrew Wood
Accounts & Human Resources - Sharon Evans
Emma Macorison - North East Commercial Manager
Publishers - Ian Merricks & Martin Dallaghan

Thanks
Joelle Asaro Berman, Laura Bowyer, Vanessa Chamberlain Machir, Chris Cox, Kate Hudson, Tim Marshall, Scott Oxley, Katy Sian

©**itchy Media Ltd**
Leeds Innovation Centre, 103 Clarendon Road, Leeds LS2 9DF
t | 0113 246 0440 f | 0113 246 0550

Whitehorse Yard, 78 Liverpool Road, London N1 0QD
t | 020 7288 4300 f | 020 7359 6001

e | Wherearemymittens@itchymedia.co.uk
www.itchycity.co.uk

ISBN: 1-903753-72-4